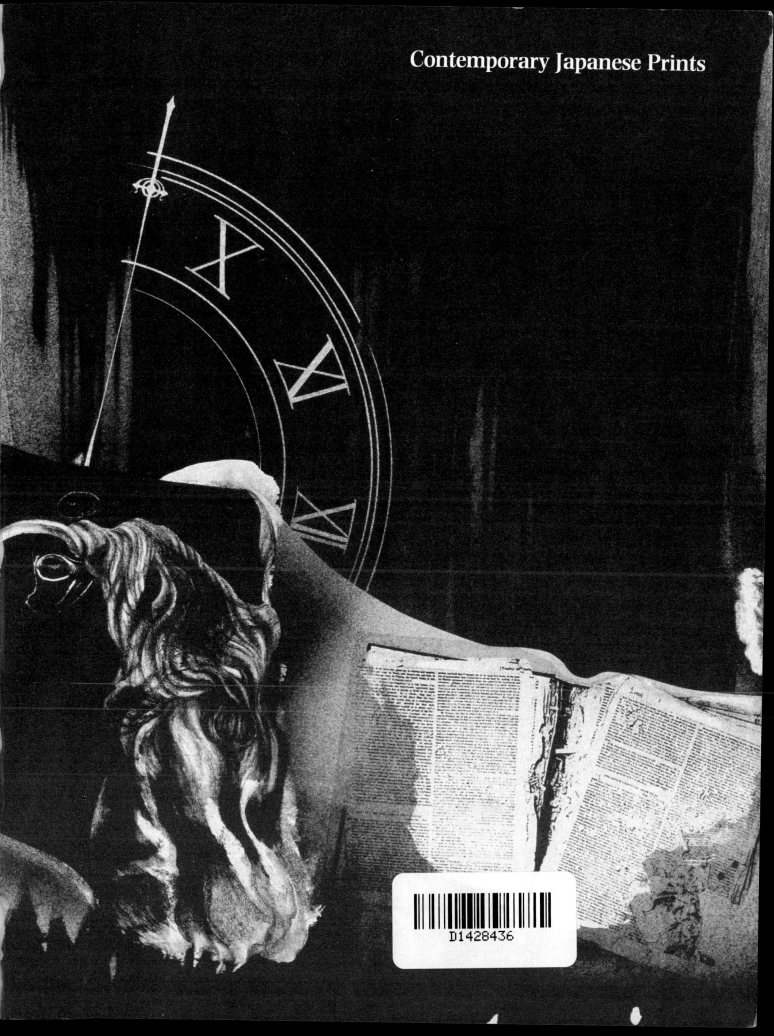

Contemporary Japanese Prints

Contemporary

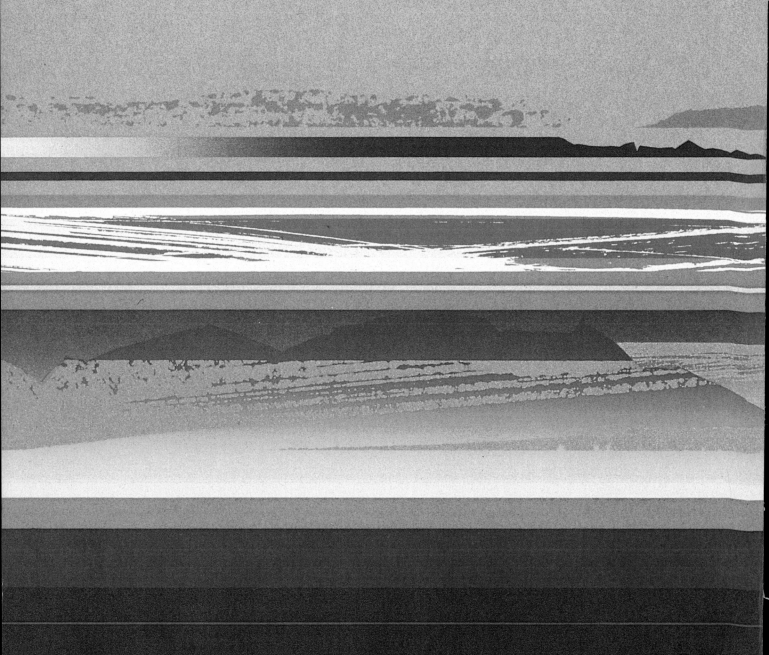

Japanese Prints

Symbols of a society in transition

LAWRENCE SMITH

Published for the Trustees of the British Museum
by British Museum Publications

© Introduction and The Prints and
the Artists, The Trustees of the British
Museum 1985
© Printmaking Techniques, CWAJ 1985
(adapted from Leslie Huff)
© Colour illustrations, CWAJ 1985

Published by British Museum Publications Ltd
46 Bloomsbury Street London WC1B 3QQ

British Library Cataloguing in Publication Data

Smith, Lawrence
    Contemporary Japanese prints: symbols of a
    society in transition.
    1. Prints, Japanese   2. Prints – 20th
    century – Japan
    I. Title
    769.952   NE771

ISBN 0 7141 1425 1

Designed by Roger Davies
Set in Photina by Southern Positives and
Negatives (SPAN), Lingfield, Surrey
and printed in Great Britain by
W. S. Cowell Ltd, Ipswich
Colour origination by Colorlito, Milan

The colour illustrations were
photographed by Takeshi Sera
The portrait photographs were supplied
by the individual artists

Exhibition dates
Hawaii Loa College, Honolulu:
9–25 September 1985
Atrium of the International Monetary Fund
Building, Washington, DC: 8–25 October 1985
Chicago Public Library Cultural Center:
15 November–28 December 1985
Pratt Graphics Center, New York City:
6 January–3 February 1986
Peabody Museum, Salem, Massachusetts:
20 February–11 August 1986
The British Museum, London:
3 September–26 October 1986

Front cover
Takeda Hideo: *Mark of the Fan* (no. 64, detail)

Back cover
Arichi Yoshito: *Space-Time 36* (no. 2)

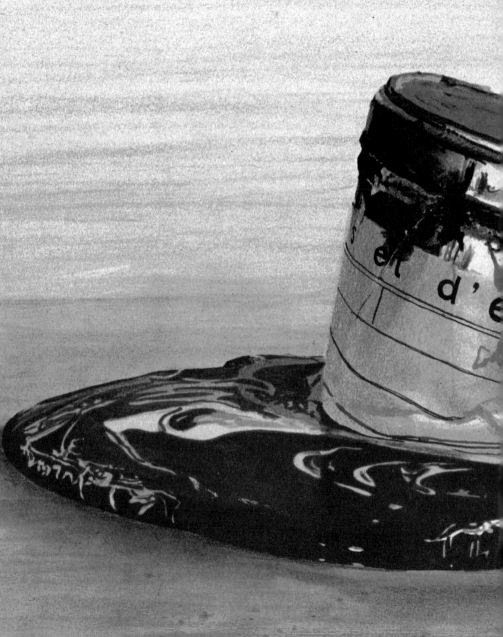

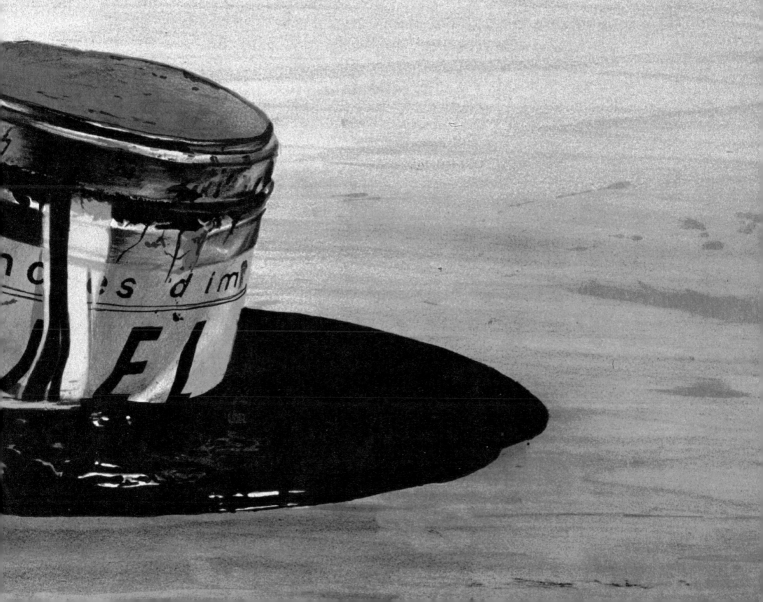

Contents

The College Women's Association of Japan and its Print Show

The College Women's Association of Japan (CWAJ) is an international organization of 700 members representing twenty-eight nationalities. Founded in 1949, this voluntary, non-profit-making organization is committed to the promotion of cross-cultural understanding. The original travel grants have long since been converted into a generously funded scholarship programme for Japanese women to study abroad at graduate level, for non-Japanese women to continue graduate study in Japan, and for visually handicapped Japanese students to pursue graduate study. The proceeds of the Print Show and an annual winter Lecture Series, both open to the public, also support a widespread and varied programme of English language assistance to Japanese teachers and students of English.

This specially selected exhibition of 80 contemporary prints was organized in 1985 to celebrate thirty years of annual Print Shows in Tokyo by CWAJ. The first exhibition and sale of prints took place in 1956 and featured 91 woodblock prints by 40 artists. Its aim was to introduce this relatively unknown art form to the foreign community in Tokyo. Since its inception, the Print Show has continued to expand in size and scope to include a variety of printmaking techniques, and in 1984 presented 229 prints by 128 artists. It is now the second largest contemporary print exhibition in Japan, and has become a noteworthy cultural event in Tokyo every October.

The mounting of the original print shows was handled by one of Tokyo's leading art galleries until 1972, when CWAJ took over the entire management of the exhibition. Since each year's committee determines policy for its exhibition, there have been many variations, but the one unchanging feature of the show has been an enthusiasm for contemporary Japanese prints. Only works originated within the preceding two years have been presented. A recent addition to the exhibition has been the work of foreign artists resident in Japan as well as Japanese artists working abroad.

Contemporary Japanese Prints: Symbols of a society in transition is additional to and separate from the annual Print Show. It has been selected by an international jury and is intended to express CWAJ's gratitude to the many artists (some forty-five of whom have appeared in CWAJ's Print Shows for more than fifteen years) who have supported the work of the association through their regular participation in its annual exhibition and sale of their works. At the same time CWAJ hopes the show will contribute to greater cross-cultural awareness by communicating the beauty and variety of late twentieth-century Japanese printmaking to art lovers in the United States and Britain. The contents of the exhibition will become a part of the British Museum's collection at the conclusion of its tour, where they will be a permanent record of a moment of artistic history in one country.

Selection Committee

TETSURŌ MUROBUSHI, Editor-in-Chief, *Hanga Geijutsu*

LAWRENCE SMITH, Keeper of Oriental Antiquities, The British Museum

ANDREW STASIK, Director, Pratt Graphics Center, New York City

The exhibition was selected in May 1985 in Tokyo, Japan

Exhibition Committee

Co-Chairmen

SHIGEKO JANET KATANO   MARION RAMSTAD

Fund Raising

EIKO SUZUKI

Publications and Video Co-ordination

REIKO NAGASE   LEE WAREHAM

Print Curators

NORIKO YAGI   SHEILA ROSENTHAL

Publicity

JUDITH CALLANDER   NORIKO SHIBA

Crating, Shipping and Insurance

MARY-JANE CONNELLY   MIYOKO YAMAZAKI

Secretary

AMY FLINT

Treasurers

EMIKO OI   SUSAN SULLIVAN

Feasibility Study

PATRICIA HERCUS   EIKO IKEDA

CWAJ President, 1985

AKIKO KUNO

Acknowledgments

This exhibition has been made possible through the generosity of the
following benefactors:

The Japan Foundation

Pfizer International Incorporated

British Airways

Northwest Orient Airlines

The project was also sponsored by the following organizations:

Chugai Pharmaceutical Company

Four Winds Japan Ltd

Fuji Xerox Company Ltd

Haniwa-kai

Kao Corporation

KDD (Japan International Telecommunications Entity)

Kikkoman Corporation

Morgan Stanley International Ltd, Tokyo

NEC Corporation

Sanyo Trading Company Ltd

Shiseido Corporation

Mr Tanemichi Sohma

Sony Corporation

Suntory Corporation

SVS Company Ltd

Takata Corporation

TELEJAPAN International Inc.

Toshiba Corporation

Toyota Motor Corporation

United Airlines

CWAJ would like to thank its overseas alumnae and friends for their indispensable
contributions in introducing CWAJ Print Shows to museums and galleries and
in arranging publicity and receptions for exhibition openings:

Boston

KATE LATHROP   MIKE MECHEM

Chicago

ANN BRENNAN   JUDY DAY

Honolulu

NANCY FORSTER

New York

MARGARET K. JOHNSON

San Francisco

JANET BAXTER   ELIZABETH CHASE

Washington, DC

BARBARA B. SELIGMANN   LILLY TSUKAHIRA

Also Dr Franz G. Geierhaas of the International Print Society for timely advice
and introductions, as well as Bunny Raabe and Marie Myerscough
1983 and 1984 CWAJ Presidents respectively.

Preface

Although I am named as author of this book, it has in reality been a pleasant task of editing material supplied mostly by other people. Many of them are members of the College Women's Association of Japan, who are acknowledged on other pages; but I should like personally to thank them all for their hard work, attention to detail and great enthusiasm, as well as for their warmth and friendship. I must here also record my appreciation of the expertise, sound judgement and good humour of my fellow jurors on the selection committee, Mr Tetsurō Murobushi and Mr Andrew Stasik. We are jointly responsible for the selection, but any errors in the text are mine alone. The opinions in the introduction and descriptions of the prints are also mine, although I have tried to be as objective as one can be when confronted with the genuinely contemporary.

As a curator of the British Museum, I must also thank the CWAJ corporately for its imaginative concept that the prints in the travelling exhibition which forms the basis of this book should at the end of the last showing become part of our permanent collections. This will preserve complete for future study a moment in the history of the art of Japan.

Most of all I very warmly thank the individual artists who have through the CWAJ given these examples of their work.

Finally, my thanks are due to those not already mentioned who have offered their help: my good friends Kyōko Andō, Rebecca Salter and Robert Vergez, and my colleagues Anthony Griffiths and Victor Harris for essential information; and Elizabeth Foxell for typing the manuscript and keeping my papers under control.

LAWRENCE SMITH
Keeper of Oriental Antiquities
The British Museum

Introduction

The subtitle of this book, *Symbols of a society in transition*, was well chosen. The eighty prints were selected from an entry of well over 200 artists; and they in turn represent perhaps less than half the print artists in Japan who are professionals, even if they do not all earn their living entirely through selling prints. That is a lot of artists in one country at one time in one artistic medium, and their works tell us much about Japan now and in the forty years since the Pacific War ended.

It is hard to deny that Japan is a society in transition. But one has to ask the questions 'How long has it been in transition?' and 'Is it different in this respect from other highly developed societies?'. The answer to the first question will take us back a long way, for in fact Japanese society has been changing at some pace since its official policy of isolation from the rest of the world ended in 1853, when the American naval commander Perry sailed into Uraga Bay. Perry brought with him the first whiff of the real power of Western technology, a power which the Japanese readily understood and soon began to adopt. Their cultural history since then has been one of continuing tension between that international and technological world, of which they have been and obviously still are prominent members, and their own very special ways and attitudes.

This leads naturally to the second question. For has not every advanced nation in fact gone through a similar process since industrialization began to take hold? And is it not indeed still going on in every such nation? If this is true, then we must ask if Japan does in fact differ, and how the prints under discussion reflect this.

Japan's unusual history since 1853 has provided a rather different situation from that of those other East Asian nations which have had a Western technology and way of life imposed on them through a mixture of force, necessity and historical inevitability. For until the end of the Pacific War in 1945, Japan deliberately chose to adopt some of the attitudes and skills of the advanced economic or colonialist powers of the West, while retaining her independence from their domination as well as much of her cultural identity. Japan was therefore at that time able to some extent to control the pace of change brought about by modernization and to integrate it with her own distinctive way of life. This process can be seen in the world of the print. Between the late 1870s, when Kobayashi Kiyochika began his experiments in reproducing the effects of light and shade through the medium of the traditional woodblock print, and the end of the Pacific War, Japanese graphic artists show on the whole a slow and relatively dignified absorption of Western artistic methods. The print movement known as *Sōsaku Hanga* ('Creative Prints') was most successful in this integration. Ono Tadashige (no. 46) is the only artist in this exhibition who is a true survivor of that pre-war school of woodblock printing, his style retaining the restraint, sobriety and warm, rich colour which already characterized his work in the 1930s.

With the Allied occupation in 1945, a completely new era began. Japan now started on a rapid transition into a democratic and economically active modern nation. Until 1952 the foreigners were not only present but also in control; and following independence, Japan had already by the mid-1960s achieved the position of one of the world's most materially advanced nations. With that process came many changes which were radically to alter the world of art. A more Americanized educational system led to a proliferation of universities, junior colleges and art schools. There were soon to be large numbers of young people training in such places and studying art there, instead of going into

N.B. All Japanese names are given with the family name first.

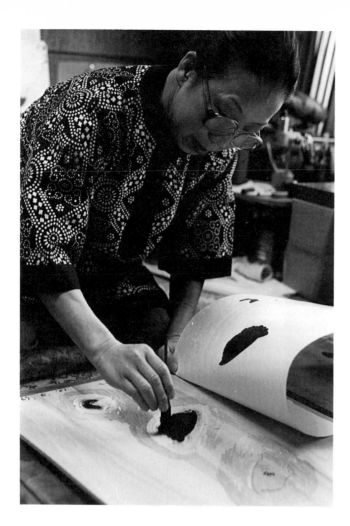
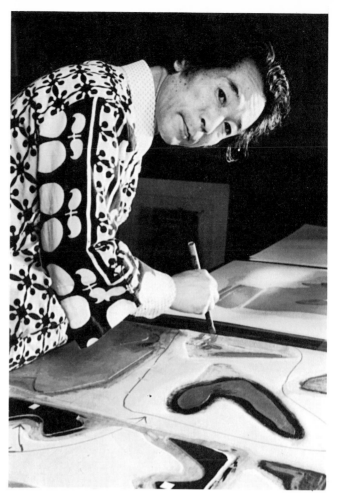

Iwami Reika (no. 14); Takahashi Rikio (no. 62)

apprenticeships in artists' or craftsmen's workshops and studios. There were as a result far more artists, and of those the proportion of printmakers gradually increased as it became possible to train and major in graphic art alone at certain schools. The college professor became the most important influence on many young individuals.

All of this resulted in a general break with the past, and an ever greater interest in the styles and techniques of the international artistic world, led since the 1950s by the USA rather than by Europe. This can be seen in the careers of some of the artists born in the 1930s and trained in the first ten years after 1945. Their works show a determined effort to come to terms with the techniques and styles of Western printmakers and painters. One of the best known is Ay-ō (no. 3), who in his early thirties adopted with great enthusiasm the cheerfully colourful Pop Art style of the USA and has kept to it ever since. Yayanagi (no. 74) is of the same generation, with much the same attitude, and so in their ways are Sawada (no. 55) and Watanabe Toyoshige (no. 70). All of these work in silkscreen, the most 'contemporary' of the print mediums (yet paradoxically one which originated in Japanese textile dyeing techniques).

But this is not the whole story by any means. This very decade 1945–1955 saw the most confident flowering of the Creative Print movement (*Sōsaku Hanga*), mentioned earlier. The major artist of this school was Onchi Kōshirō (1891–1955), whose style reached its finest expression at that time under the much freer artistic climate which then developed after years of nationalist censorship. His achievement was to integrate an almost pure abstraction, ultimately derived from European example, with a truly Japanese aesthetic of tone and texture, and to express it through woodblocks cut and printed by himself. This was one of the ideals of the school, though it was not always kept to. As a direct tradition *Sōsaku Hanga* was to decline sharply in fashion within Japan in the 1960s under the enthusiasm for the genuinely foreign, but many of its artists remained loyal to their style and to Onchi's ideals, and have continued to produce fine work up to the present day. In this book they are represented, apart from Ono Tadashige (no. 46) who was working before the Pacific War, by Iwami (no. 14), Maki (no. 33) and Takahashi (no. 62).

At the same time, some older printmakers were still working in different styles and techniques directly related to specifically Japanese traditions. The stencil-prints of Watanabe Sadao (no. 69) and Mori Yoshitoshi (no. 41) are in the mainstream of the Japanese Folk Art movement which had been at its height in the 1920s and 1930s, and which in Munakata (d. 1975) produced Japan's most famous twentieth-century artist. And the Yoshida family of Tokyo continued to produce their woodblocks of landscape and townscape, as they had done since the early 1920s, and still do, though they have now diversified in subject and even technique (nos 75, 76 and 77). Even in the field of pure European abstraction, Murai (no. 42) was carrying on a dignified and in its way solid and traditional style. The outward-looking tumults of the generation coming to maturity in the 1960s, then, were heavily counter-balanced by an older and more Japanese tendency which was eventually to help produce a greater sense of integration.

In woodblock, the most traditional medium of all, there emerged during the 1960s several artists who were to contribute to this reintegration. One of the most important is Kurosaki (no. 30). He is important not only because of the imaginative power of his prints, but also because he was one of the first to

Kurosaki Akira (no. 30)

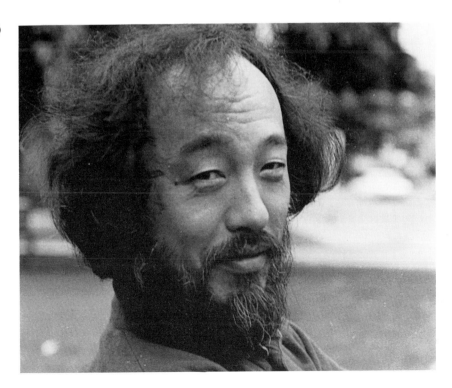

produce work in an entirely international style (in his case, a variation of 'psychedelic' art) in a completely traditional medium: his prints are produced to his designs from woodblocks, but actually printed by an associate craftsman who works in his studio. This is a partial reversion to a practice which flourished in Japan for centuries before the *Sōsaku Hanga* movement declared that an artist should carry out all the cutting and printing processes himself, and it was indeed this more co-operative earlier method that produced all the great *Ukiyoe* prints of the eighteenth and nineteenth centuries.

Kurosaki was not the only artist of his generation to produce interesting new work in woodblock. Others are Maeda (no. 32), who studied with Onchi's pupil Yamaguchi Gen, and Matsumoto (no. 34). Perhaps even more interesting are the contorted and energetic black and white prints, extremely sculptural in inspiration, of Tomihari (no. 66). But noticeably it is the artists born after the Pacific War who have returned to woodblock with increasing enthusiasm,

Kawachi Seikō (no. 19)

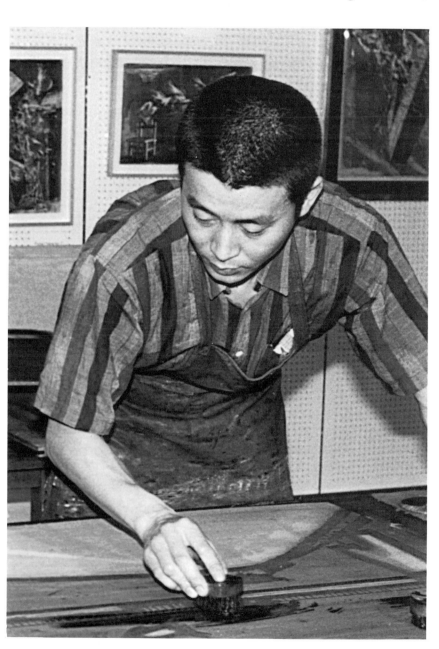

14

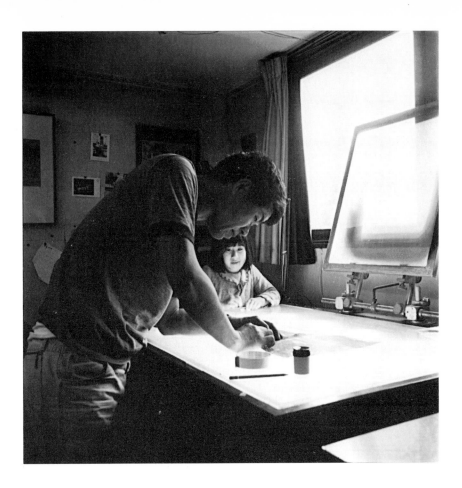

Noda Tetsuya (no. 45)

since coming to maturity in the late 1970s. Their leader has been Kawachi (no. 19), an artist who has begun to be as appreciated by connoisseurs outside Japan as is the older Kurosaki, and for some of the same reasons. Kawachi's great visions of urban tension and stress gain much of their strength from his excited use of the woodblock surface. Unlike Kurosaki, he does his own printing, using the traditional baren pad to rub the impression from the block into the paper. In this sense, his prints are more 'individual', especially in the differences between pulls of the same edition, and are a return in a more modern form to the ideals of the Creative Print movement.

Kawachi's inspiration, and that of his contemporary Morozumi Ozamu (b.1949), has breathed new enthusiasm into those younger artists who are now using woodblock with more variety than ever before. This is no doubt a good development, for it puts them back in touch with the technique which had been by far the most important one used in Japan from the early seventeenth century. Those illustrated are Matsushita (no. 36), Mori Hidefumi (no. 39), Yamanaka (no. 72), Yoshida Ayomi (no. 75) and Zhang (no. 79): these prints impress by the extraordinary range they cover in the one medium, an indication that woodblock may now be gaining in popularity as its wider possibilities are increasingly explored. The work of Zhang, who was born outside Japan, is a particularly interesting example of the range of texture and tone which can still be found in the ancient technique.

Woodblock also plays a part in the work of Noda (no. 45), the most internationally admired of all the younger Japanese printmakers working today. If at first sight it seems a minor part, yet it is an essential one. Without their dead-white woodblock-printed backgrounds, his photographic black images produced through a silkscreen would lack that distancing from the merely personal which makes them so much more effective than their imitations by lesser artists. Noda has added a dimension to the ancient East Asian tradition of painting in black ink on a white surface. In that tradition, the black is thought of as positive (*yang* in Chinese) and the white as negative (*yin*). By adding the white as well as the black (on a beige paper) Noda in effect provides two positives.

Noda's awareness of other techniques comes from his teaching at the print-making department of Tokyo University of Fine Arts, where all the contemporary methods are available and good artists are consistently produced in all of them (nos 4, 9, 11, 22, 36, 43, 45, 60, 67, 72, 79). Nevertheless, the most important work in contemporary graphics to have come from that school has been in the intaglio techniques of which Nakabayashi (no. 43) is such a distinguished teacher and practitioner.

Since the seventeenth century, when the Europeans first introduced etching and engraving to Japan, these intaglio methods in black and white have always been thought of as the most foreign and different, and they have to a lesser extent continued to be thought of in that way, even after they became much more available in the second half of the nineteenth century, together with their later developments of aquatint and mezzotint. The most important reason for their slow rate of absorption may have been that they are all by nature methods of expressing light and shade, which played little part in the traditional schools of Japanese painting. They therefore remained a minority and exotic interest until the post-war proliferation of colleges offering a Westernized art curriculum made their basic precepts commonplace and

Nakabayashi Tadayoshi (no. 43)

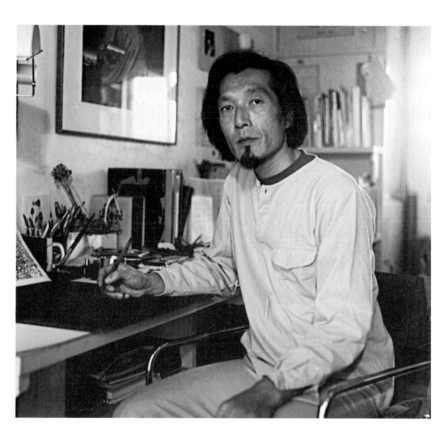

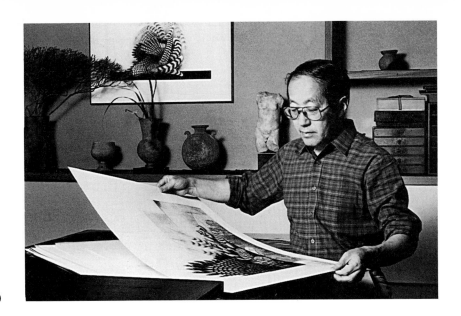

Suda Toshio (no. 61)

acceptable. The older generation of intaglio printmakers, like Hamaguchi Yōzō (b.1909), had trained in Europe or the USA, and none of them achieved much recognition until after 1950. But after that date, etching and related metal-plate techniques began to become associated with a foreignness based on the example of the USA. They were no longer a minority interest and had become both respectable and desirable.

Although a less well-known intaglio artist than Hamaguchi or Hamada Chimei (b.1917), the instrument of much of this change was Komai Tetsurō (b.1920), who taught later in his career at Tokyo University of Fine Arts and was the master of Nakabayashi, who has continued his work, and of many others. The result has been, especially since 1970, an amazing burst of enthusiastic work in these old techniques which had seemed to have lost much of their impetus in their original homes in Europe and North America. The work of Nakabayashi himself shows an interesting progression from a Westernized use of etching to a more complex technique, producing a depth of surface which is recognizably Japanese in its feeling for texture and a use of black and white drifting back to the ideals of ink painting.

It is perhaps not surprising that intaglio techniques, which work from the dark to the light, should now have become the recognized medium for work of sombre meaning. There are a number illustrated – the mysterious constructions of Kobayashi Jinan (no. 25), the enigmatic assemblages of Yamanobe (no. 73), and the jokey but disturbing extravaganzas of Sakuma (no. 54) and Suda (no. 61). Most impressive of all in their sense of controlled menace are Shiroki's mezzotints of melting and incandescent steel (no. 59). This seems to be a fruitful field for artists who wish to express the darker sides of existence, a subject which had no ready outlet in the more traditional art of East Asia except for occasional outbursts of high-spirited *diablerie*. It is most noticeable that direct depiction of human suffering, grief, violence or degradation remains a rare phenomenon in the Japanese print, though it receives more popular expression in cartoon form, both in newspapers and magazines and on television.

Those artists who have moved from pure black and white intaglio to the more technically time-consuming coloured forms of etching, aquatint and mezzotint have tended to be less sombre if not always less enigmatic. Here the sheer delight in the sensuality of technique can become the main reason for the print, an attitude not dissimilar to some of the dazzling brushwork displays of the nineteenth-century Shijō school of painting. The super-romantic revellings in intense black and red mezzotint of Saitō Kaoru (no. 51) are the most remarkable of those illustrated. Others revel in subtle tonal and surface contrasts of greater abstraction, such as Sahashi (no. 50) and Umezawa (no. 67). Only Ikeda Ryōji in this book uses colour intaglio as a means of heightening unease (no. 12), while Kuroda (no. 29) uses it in quite the opposite way to lighten his atmosphere of runaway frenzy.

Speculation about future directions in Japanese printmaking is interesting but likely to be wrong. The rapid decline of *Sōsaku Hanga* after 1960 is an example of a trend expected by very few people, although the seeds of its decline had been sown in the educational changes of the previous decade, as described earlier. At the moment, intaglio processes are dominant – twenty-six out of our eighty illustrations are intaglio (including one wood-engraving) and three others combine it with a contrasting technique. It does seem at present that younger artists are feeling more and more confident in this field, and there is some evidence that they are beginning to use it to express a more traditionally based sensibility in black and white, drawing on the many centuries of austere ink painting and calligraphy which are an inescapable part of Japan's artistic heritage. Nakabayashi (no. 43), Shinkai (no. 57) and Umezawa (no. 67) are good examples of that tendency.

The future of lithography in Japan, however, is much less certain. This, the fourth of the major processes (they are all described on pp. 20–25), is the least found among the selection illustrated in this book (which is in itself quite adequately representative of current trends). Lithography has two great strengths. One is its ability to produce a brilliantly finished and smooth surface (nos 9, 27, 35, 60 and 68, for example) and in that respect it resembles silkscreen. In reproduction the two may be indistinguishable. The flat polish of these works derives from models further west, and that so far has been their attraction. It is possible to speculate that their lack of texture may lead Japanese printmakers back in larger numbers to the woodblock and intaglio techniques with their greater potential for depth. It is worth noting that Japan's most distinguished silkscreen artist, Noda Tetsuya (no. 45), has sought to achieve that depth by the addition of woodblock and the careful choice of textured paper.

On the other hand, there are factors peculiar to the present (1985) which may tend to the retention of the highly polished products of lithograph and silkscreen. One is the enthusiasm for them among foreign markets, especially in the USA. Artists like Ay-ō (no. 3), Endō (no. 6), Hara (no. 9) and Sawada (no. 55) cannot afford to ignore their many admirers overseas. Second is their popularity with interior designers. Prints have become a recognized way of decorating modern interiors not only abroad but also in Japan itself, where city apartments are always multiplying. In fact, the concentration of printmakers in great cities is simply a reflection of the urbanization of Japan on a much greater scale. It is an almost startling fact that of the eighty artists in this book, thirty-seven live in Tokyo and a further nineteen in the adjacent suburbanized prefectures of Kanagawa, Saitama and Chiba, while only four (apart from those few residing overseas) live more than a few hours' journey from the great cities of the main island – Tokyo, Osaka, Nagoya, Kyoto and Yokohama.

As a result, the urban environment is the setting for the lives of most of these artists: and the slickness of the graphic worlds of television, advertising and magazines – brightly coloured, polished, often sardonic – is all around them. It is to be doubted that these influences can be ignored and play no part in future graphics. But, as we have already said, the darker side of life in cities – the sense of claustrophobia, the stress, the neurosis, the lack of warm human contact – may have to continue to find a more oblique outlet in the surrealist, abstract and expressionist styles well suited to intaglio.

Of course, Japan is far from isolated, even if there is some evidence for an increasing self-confidence in her culture, which is in itself a natural result of her very great material success. Japanese artists go abroad to study in ever greater numbers – especially to Paris, San Francisco, Los Angeles and New York – and there continue to be influenced by new and old foreign styles, techniques and environments. It is here that the other strength of lithography is most in evidence, for it remains the most important technique in the USA and Europe, especially for painters who wish also to do prints which are very close to their original work. But lithograph is flat – even flatter than silkscreen – and it is ultimately best suited to those printmakers who wish to express ideas, pure design or pure colour. As we have several times hinted, this two-dimensional approach is one which is ill suited to the more native Japanese tradition of an appreciation of surface, texture and material.

It would be misleading, too, to underestimate the effect of the presence of foreign artists working in Japan. In this book, there are six who do so or have done so for long periods (nos 15, 31, 44, 49, 79 and 80). Such resident foreign artists are not as directly influential as they once were when Japan was absorbing the techniques and styles of the international world. But they all provide, owing to the extreme self-consciousness of the Japanese people, an indirect influence by showing what effects their culture has on people outside it. It should be mentioned here that in the most traditional technique of cutting cherry-wood blocks for printing (as opposed to the larger veneered blocks used by artists like Kawachi) there are now almost as many foreign artists as native Japanese. Included among them are Clifton Karhu (b.1927), Daniel Kelly (b.1947), Joshua Rome (b.1953), Ted Colyer (b.1947) and Sarah Brayer (b.1957). If the traditional craftsmen printing in this style in Kyoto and Tokyo continue to decline in numbers, we may see a future when this oldest of Japanese graphic techniques is mainly in the hands of foreign practitioners. In Japanese art, the future is even more fascinating than the present or past.

This explanation, however brief, should be enough to show that these contemporary prints are indeed symbols (but not the only ones) of a society in transition, and that, as is always true in Japan, these processes are deeply affected by very strong native cultural and social factors which change much less quickly than the more superficial and volatile technological scene. The cover of this book illustrates very neatly these complexities. It is encouraging, nevertheless, to look through these prints and enjoy their variety and vitality. The energy, enthusiasm, imagination and craftsmanship which they show are indeed symbols of Japan today. Their ambiguous and sometimes confused and confusing relations with the art of the rest of the international world are likely in the next decade to become more complex still.

Printmaking Techniques

Adapted from Leslie Huff's text for the CWAJ Print Show Catalogue, 1983

The common techniques for making prints can conveniently be divided into four main types – intaglio, relief, planographic, and screen.

I The Intaglio Process

Definition
The depressed surfaces of the printing medium, usually a metal plate, print the image when the paper is pressed into them. 'Intaglio' is of Italian derivation, meaning 'I cut into'.

Process
The image is drawn onto a metal plate (copper, zinc, brass, aluminium, magnesium or steel) and then incised. The depressed areas are filled with an oil-based ink while the non-printing surface is wiped clean. A press forces the dampened paper into the depressed areas, and the image is transferred. An embossed intaglio print is pressed without ink.

Variations

Sharp tool incisor

ENGRAVING A square or lozenge-shaped tool, called a burin, is used to incise fine lines into a metal plate. The printed lines are crisp and sharp. This technique is rarely used by contemporary artists in Japan.

DRYPOINT The point of a needle of hardened steel is scratched across a metal plate, displacing the metal and creating a fragile groove and burr. The printed lines are soft and heavy.

MEZZOTINT A rocker or wide heavy chisel with a curved and serrated cutting edge is used to roughen a metal plate. In this state, the plate prints a solid black, but it is burnished and scraped with areas which will remain white, or tones from white through to nearly black. The effect is lustrous, with a strong sense of light and shade.

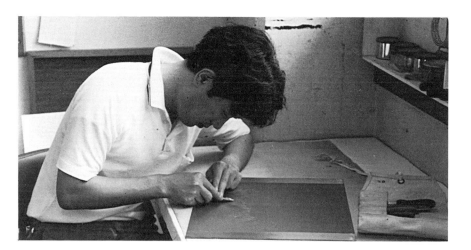

Umezawa Kazuo (no. 67) preparing a mezzotint plate

Acid solution incisor

ETCHING A metal plate coated with an acid-resistant substance (called a ground) is drawn upon with a needle. Set into an acid bath, the exposed image areas on the plate are eaten into. The length of time in and strength of the bath determine the width and depth of the lines. The remaining ground is removed with a solvent. A 'hard' ground is more resistant than a 'soft' ground. The finish is similar to engraving, but with a wider range of delicate effects.

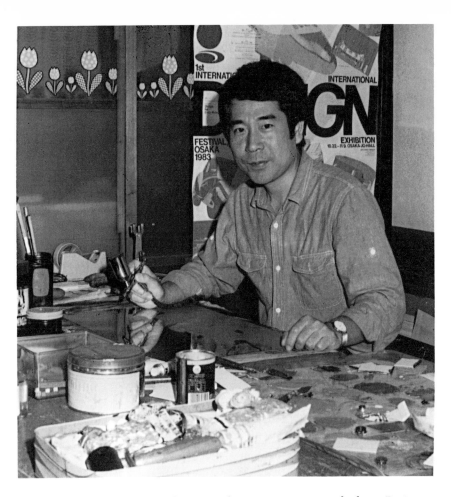

Sakuma Yoshiaki (no. 54) working on a plate

AQUATINT A method of etching tonal areas onto a metal plate. Resin or asphaltum powder is dusted onto a clean plate and affixed to the plate by heat. Set into an acid bath, the surface is roughened around each acid-resistant particle; this leaves a 'textured' surface when printed.

Other methods

COLLAGRAPH AND METAL COLLAGE The surfaces of the plate are built up with glue and other materials and printed as an intaglio process.

PHOTOGRAVURE The image is placed on the plate by photographic means using carbon tissue, a gelatin-coated paper that can be made light-sensitive.

Identification

An embossed edge caused by the weight of the press encloses the image.

2 The Relief Process

Definition

The raised surfaces of the printing medium, usually a woodblock, print the image areas.

Process

The image is drawn in freehand or traced onto a block. The non-image areas are carved and chiselled away and the raised surfaces are inked. A sheet of dampened paper is laid on the block and rubbed from behind with a burnisher to transfer the inked image to the paper.

Multi-coloured relief prints usually necessitate the carving, inking, and printing of a separate block for each colour. Artists employ several systems of registration to ensure the perfect alignment of each block, so that colours do not overlap, or overlap deliberately to achieve special effects.

Variations

WOODBLOCK, LINOCUT, EMBOSSED PLASTER The raised printing surface is created by the carving and chiselling away of the non-image background areas of a woodblock, linoleum block or plaster block respectively.

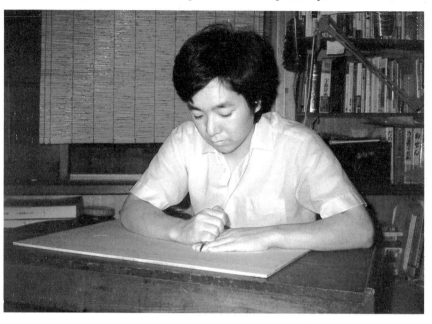

Yamanaka Gen (no. 72) cutting a woodblock

WOOD ENGRAVING The raised printing surface is created by carving away or incising the image areas of a cross-grain woodblock so that the non-image areas serve as the printing surface. The hard cross-grain allows small fine lines and patterns.

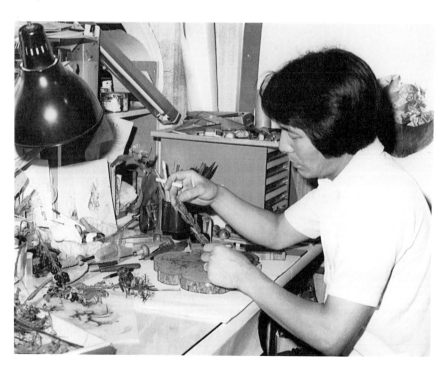

Kobayashi Keisei (no. 26) with a cross-grain woodblock for a wood engraving

METAL OR CARDBOARD RELIEF The raised printing surface is constructed by building up a metal plate or sheet of cardboard.

Contemporary Japanese and Western woodblock processes compared

	JAPANESE	WESTERN
Block	plywood sheet	any hard or soft wood
Ink, pigment	water-based natural pigments and rice paste (sometimes oil-based)	oil-based
Ink application	brush moved in circular motion	brayer rolled across the surface
Paper	dampened Japanese	dampened Japanese
Registration	*Kentō* system of corner and side-edge notches in block	right angle T-square at corner
Burnisher	baren (disk of coiled rope encased in bamboo skin)	baren, or other flat instrument

Identification
Discernible circular textures of the burnisher.
Discernible graining of the woodblock.
Influence of the woodgrain on curvilinear images.
Feelable edge to areas of pigment, caused by light pressure of the burnisher.

3 The Planographic Process

Definition
The surface of the printing medium is entirely flat. Almost all planographic prints are called *lithographs.*

Process
A stone or metal plate (usually zinc or aluminium) is roughened, or grained, to ensure it will hold an image upon it. The image is either freely drawn, transferred manually or photographically, or airbrushed onto the surface with a form of 'tusche', a compound of wax, tallow, soap, shellac and lampblack. The entire surface is coated twice with a gum arabic and acid solution, called an etch, so that the greasy image area will hold ink or pigment rolled across it,

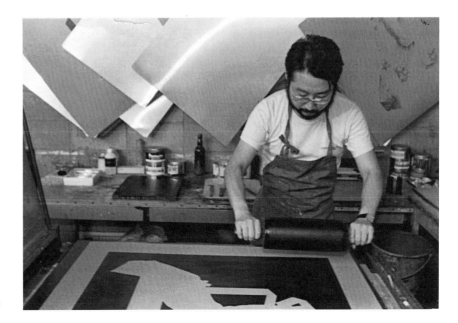

Wako Syūji (no. 68) inking a lithographic plate

and the clean background area will accept water. Paper, either dampened or dry, when applied under pressure to the surface, picks up the inked image.

Shading is dependent upon the application of the tusche, the acidity of and time allotted to the etch, and the viscosity of the ink.

A multi-colour lithograph demands accurate registration since only one colour can be printed at a time. Many systems are used, including pinholes, T-bar markings and cut-out windows.

Variation

OFFSET LITHOGRAPHY A technique used mainly for mass reproduction, where the image is first taken from the plate by a rubber roller, and then transferred to the paper.

Identification

The spontaneity of the imagery, reflecting very closely the artist's hand.
Watery or crayon textures.
Absence of plate marks or embossments.

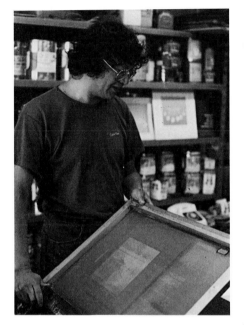

Shimizu Momo (no. 56) with a silkscreen

4 The Screen Process

Definition

The surface of the printing medium is a fabric screen of silk (silkscreen), nylon or polyester. This supports a stencil which serves as a blockout for the passage of ink through the non-image areas of the screen. Serigraphy is a grander word for silkscreen printing.

Process

A squeegee pulled across the screen forces ink through the image areas left open by the stencil and onto the paper beneath.

Variations

Direct

NEGATIVE The stencil is created by the artist's freehand application of a blockout made of either water-soluble glue, lacquer or shellac directly onto the screen. The image is developed by the drawing of the non-image areas.

POSITIVE The stencil is developed using two substances whose solvents are incompatible with one another. First a positive image is drawn onto the screen with a soluble pigment, which is then completely overpainted with an insoluble one. When dry, a solvent is used to remove the first underlying substance and expose the image areas, leaving the non-image areas impervious to the action of the squeegee. Common positive methods include glue/shellac, glue/lacquer, tusche/glue, litho crayon/glue, and rubber cement/glue.

Indirect

NEGATIVE The image is created by making a negative stencil of another material and affixing it to the screen. Common materials include paper, thin plastic, thin brass or copper plates, hand-cut lacquer stencil film and hand-cut water-soluble film.

POSITIVE The image is created using photographic processes. A positive image, which is made from either a photographic positive or a hand-drawn opaque image on transparent acetate, is placed on a special sensitized film or against a screen coated with a sensitized emulsion. Wherever light travels through the positive, the sensitized coating hardens while the unexposed areas dissolve and become the open printing areas. The light-sensitive emulsion may be applied to the screen directly or indirectly via a separate sensitized sheet of film.

Identification
Seeming thickness of the ink gives a sense of the image lying on top of the paper.
Bright, sharply defined edges, or fluid painterly effects.
Under close scrutiny, the texture of the screen can often be made out.

5 Combination Processes

Contemporary artists often use combinations of the processes to widen their range of effects. As will be seen from the descriptions of the prints illustrated in this book, combinations have become common and they are likely to increase as large numbers of graphic artists seek individual expression.

One of the commonest combinations is the use of *embossing* with other techniques. Usually the paper is embossed before pigments are applied. This effect can be achieved by an intaglio plate or by a relief surface: in both cases, the shape is embossed into the thick paper without the use of ink or pigment. This technique is a traditional one in Japanese woodblock printing, and continues to be much used. Thick, traditionally produced Japanese hand-made papers are particularly suited to it.

This desire for variety is also leading to the invention of unique personal techniques by individual artists. These techniques are often so unusual that it is not possible to guess from the finished print how it was produced, and the only way of discovering is to ask the artist.

The Prints and the Artists

NOTE ON EDITIONS AND TERMINOLOGY

A print is a way of transferring an artistic image from one medium to another, usually from a plate or block or through a screen onto paper. It is not necessarily reproductive, and it is possible for only *one* print to be made, as an original work of art. However, most artists produce a print in an edition, numbered from one up to the total planned. This total is usually chosen in advance, so that for an edition of, say, one hundred, the artist will mark his or her first prints 1/100, 2/100 and so on up to 100/100. The existence of a print numbered, say, 55/100 does not mean that all of the hundred have been printed. Many artists take an impression only when an order is received, and this may extend over many years. Sometimes an edition is never fully printed and if the blocks are still in existence when the artist dies they are sometimes used to take reprints. These will not, of course, bear the artist's signature. It is considered normal to destroy or deface blocks or plates when the edition is completed, but this does not always happen; and in the most traditional circles of printing on cherry-wood blocks, where the cutter and printer usually differ from the artist, it rarely happens at all.

In Japan there has been from the early twentieth century an ideal of the 'Creative Print', conceived and produced by the artist alone. But in practice this has not always happened either, and it has at no time been followed by everyone. Some artists do everything themselves; others delegate parts of the process to others. Many lithograph artists use a professional lithographic printing workshop to take their impressions, exactly as in Europe or North America, and some silkscreen artists work in the same way. Given all this, the term 'original print' can only be defined as one designed and conceived by the artist as a print from the beginning, whatever the subsequent processes and divisions of labour. All the prints in this book are in that sense 'original'.

Outside the main edition, an artist may produce or allow to be produced other impressions, which may appear on the market and are normally of equally high standard. They are:

ARTIST'S PROOFS (*abbreviated to* A.P., E.A. *or sometimes* E.P.)

A group of impressions, not usually exceeding about 10 per cent of the edition, retained by the artist for his or her own purposes. They may be kept, given away, or sold if the main edition sells out and there is a pressing demand.

BON A TIRER PROOFS

The first impression considered good enough for the public; i.e. 'good to take' the impressions.

PRESENTATION PROOFS

Impressions specially made to give personally, often with a dedication to the recipient inscribed on the print.

PRINTER'S PROOFS (P.P.)

Impressions allocated for the personal use of the printer (when one is used).

There are also various sorts of trial proofs produced by the artist or printer during the development and perfecting of a print; but these will not normally come on the market until an artist is so eminent that the study of his or her methods becomes part of art-historical research.

Whether the artist carries out all the processes or not, it is normal with an original print, as defined above, for him or her to sign and number all the impressions personally in pencil. But like all matters to do with prints, this is not a universal rule. Some of the Creative Print artists, like Ono Tadashige, attached a slip to the back (which can, of course, become detached). And sometimes an impression seems simply to get overlooked and remain unsigned.

1 AMANO Junji (b.1949)

Edge 85-K-9
1985. 8/20
Silkscreen/embossing. 570 × 845 mm

The artist was born in Kanagawa Prefecture to the south-west of Tokyo, where he still lives, and graduated from Tama University of Fine Arts. That school has produced several artists with a very strong leaning towards texture and surface excitement, including Funasaka (no. 7), Kawachi (no. 19), Kuroda (no. 29) and Mori Hidefumi (no. 39). Amano shares in this tradition, but the rather polished elegance of this print most recalls the carefully produced surfaces of Funasaka. The 'edges' and the round spots are embossed partly from the front and partly from the back, so that the artist produces a varied texture within his abstracted design, which in reproduction may appear only a flat pattern of screen-printed celadon greens.

2 ARICHI Yoshito (b.1949)

Space-Time 36
1985. Artist's proof (main edition of 30)
Colour aquatint/embossing. 510 × 405 mm

Arichi was born in Hiroshima Prefecture and now lives in Tokyo. He studied under the Surrealist printmaker Yamanobe Yoshio (no. 73) at Nihon University, and also in England. His elegant abstract prints on the subjects of space and time use ellipses, recalling the orbits of stars and planets, set against squares and lozenges suggesting the basic relationships of geometry. The artist uses the smooth and delicate surface achievable by the colour aquatint process as if to emphasize the purity of these concepts, but in this print he contrasts it with an almost rugged embossing of the unprinted paper in the lower part of the design. The result is a telling confrontation between the world of theory and the physical world in which the artist works.

3 AY-Ō (b.1931)

Sumō Wrestling
1984. 11/120
Silkscreen. 400 × 825 mm

The artist who calls himself Ay-ō (the name is written with two obscure Chinese characters) was born in Ibaragi Prefecture, graduated from Tokyo University of Education and now lives in Tokyo. A prolific painter and printmaker, he has become internationally celebrated since his periods of residence in the USA in the 1960s, where he was heavily influenced by the Pop Art movement. His silkscreen prints, a sort of continuing celebration of the rainbow, are close to his large easel-paintings done in acrylic. Very often they are abstract, but here he has produced a fantasy based on Japan's national sport of Sumō; it is also based on a woodblock print by the nineteenth-century artist Utagawa Kunisada (1786–1864), whose signature 'Kōchōrō Kunisada Ga' is just visible in the bottom right-hand corner. Ay-ō also does etchings of far more subdued colour.

4 AZUMAYA Takemi (b.1948)

A Solar Eclipse I
1984. 15/35
Lithograph. 510 × 700 mm

The artist was born in Japan's northernmost province of Hokkaidō and studied at Tokyo University of Fine Arts, which has for a generation produced many of Japan's finest printmakers (see nos 11, 36, 43, 45, 72 and 79). Although lithography is a planographic technique, Azumaya has produced in this rich, glowing print a remarkable sense of texture by the skilful use of different colour-printings. The feeling of depth thus achieved contributes to an atmosphere which suggests mystery. It can be argued that Azumaya is here sharing in the old Japanese tradition of using subtle surface and colours. This tradition did not, until after 1945, play much part in prints, which were until then mostly representational, but it had long existed in textiles, ceramics, paper, wood and even metalwork.

5 BABA Kashiō (b.1927)

Frog and Hand
1985. 2/20
Woodblock/etching/embossing
460 × 660 mm

The title on the print is in Japanese only. Baba leaves it uncertain whether the hand is the bird-like object to the right or the raised hand of the Sumō wrestler. Like much of Baba's work, this is a cheerful satire on the confusion he sees in contemporary Japanese society, dominated by noise, a frantic desire for novelty, entertainment and adventure, and at the same time a rather disjointed appreciation of Japan's cultural past. This lack of coherence is expressed by the apparently random placing of modern and traditional subjects – the space rocket marked 'USA', the jumping jack, the cyclist, the wrestler – on a gaudy background.

The artist was born in Tokyo and educated there at Waseda High School, but now lives in Yokohama, which for well over a century has been a centre of Japanese foreign contacts.

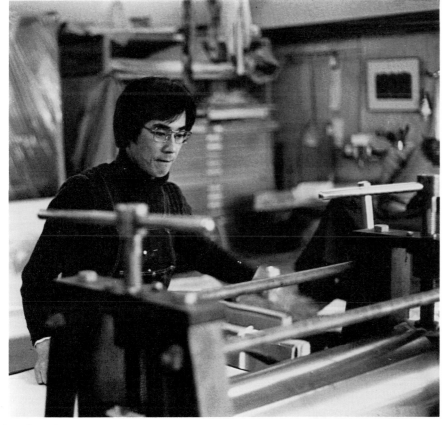

Arichi Yoshito

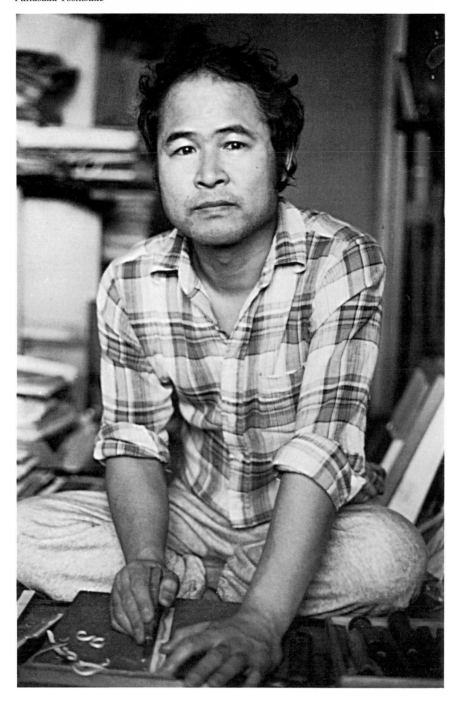

7 FUNASAKA Yoshisuke (b.1939)

My Space and My Dimension 857
1984. 9/30
Woodblock/silkscreen. 590 × 560mm

Funasaka was born in Gifu Prefecture. He was educated at Tama University of Fine Arts in Tokyo, and still lives in the metropolis. His prints usually have the same title with a serial number, and in this way he dissuades his viewers from looking for explicit meaning. Instead they can concentrate on his world of pure form, an austere and even restricted world of similar shapes which reveals great subtleties on close scrutiny. More than many in this book, Funasaka loses in reproduction the interplay of his surfaces. In this print, for example, there is a sheen of mica-dust on the large blue and rust areas, which shift with the light, while the smaller and more brightly coloured shapes, which appear in all Funasaka's prints, remain as fixed points. It is these shapes which he prints by woodblock, having devised his own method of mounting them separately so that they can be rearranged without carving a complete block.

8 HAMANISHI Katsunori (b.1949)

Opposition – Work No. 13
1984. 8/50
Mezzotint. 360 × 600mm

Hamanishi was born in Hokkaidō, studied at Tōkai University, Tokyo, and now lives in Kanagawa Prefecture. His most important influence was Yamanobe Yoshio (no. 73), whose rather sinister mezzotints have clearly left their mark on the work of the younger artist. Hamanishi is one of the many young artists in Japan today who have explored the rich, dark, three-dimensional effects possible with the old European mezzotint technique. He uses these to express the 'opposition' of polished steel tubes lashed together with old-fashioned-looking cords, a contrast perhaps of the old and the new bound together in high tension. Hamanishi's attitude to his prints is similar to that of another young artist, Kobayashi Jinan (no. 25).

6 ENDŌ Susumu (b.1933)

Space and Space – Newspaper
1984. 2/75
Offset lithograph. 450 × 450mm

The title does not appear on the print itself. Endō was born in Yamanashi Prefecture, was educated at Kuwazawa Design School and now lives in Tokyo. In order to give a specially contemporary gloss to his very contemporary images, the artist uses computer-enhanced offset lithography, similar in technique to that used in magazines and newspapers. In contrast with standard lithography, which is the process able most accurately to reproduce the actual flavour of an artist's brushwork or line, the newer variation of the process depersonalizes the image – an effect very evident in this print, with its subject of international uniformity. Endō does not identify this reader of one of Japan's several English-language daily newspapers, who seems to be isolated in an almost anonymous and literally faceless world of man-made surfaces and unnatural pink and green light.

9 HARA Takeshi (b.1942)

Strokes 85-1
1985. 36/60
Lithograph. 570 × 760mm

Hara was born in Nagoya and now lives in Tokyo. He was trained at the Tokyo University of Fine Arts. Since the early 1970s he has endlessly explored the possible variations of one motif, which he calls 'strokes'. They are done in an extraordinary range of subtle colours, often involving many different printings, and in this case a silvery dust is used to give extra lustre. Hara's prints have appealed greatly to interior decorators, especially in Japan itself, but their artistic motivation comes of course from the calligraphy of East Asia, which is such a strong influence on all Japan's culture. The gradations of the strokes and the finesse of their changes of direction directly recall the movements of brush and ink in writing the Chinese characters still used to express the Japanese language.

10 HIRONAGA Takehiko (b.1935)

Ōuda (1)

1985. 17/40
Woodblock. 450 × 695 mm

Hironaga was born in the northern prefecture of Fukushima, where he still lives, and was educated at the Tōhoku Technical High School of Nihon University. His prints are very traditional in their woodblock technique, and his work depicts mainly the old country dwellings (*minka*) which abound particularly in northern Japan and which are being destroyed in large numbers. The print shows the village of Ōuda in Nara Prefecture. The board by the shop is advertising the mountain arrowroot produced in the Yoshino district. The colour blocks have been very quietly and carefully shaded off, a difficult and subtle technique, to give a sense of depth and recession. The tiny figure at the end of the street, almost unnoticed, focuses the whole composition and brings the otherwise empty scene to life.

11 HOSHINO Michiko (b.1934)

Babel the Library; Sand the Book

1985. 4/30
Lithograph. 550 × 630 mm

The title is a translation of the Japanese, which is not inscribed on the print itself. The artist was born in Tokyo, where she still lives, and was one of that productive middle generation associated with Tokyo University of Fine Arts in the 1950s. Hoshino is unusual among them in using lithography for her surrealistic compositions, rather than etching or mezzotint. Indeed, this print seems almost to be imitating the effects of black and white mezzotint. If the sources of inspiration are clearly European pre-war Surrealism, there is nevertheless an individual dark intensity in this image of international unease.

12 IKEDA Ryōji (b.1947)

Within

1984. 14/35
Etching/aquatint. 490 × 490 mm

The title is written on the back of the print only. Ikeda lives in Tokyo, but was born in

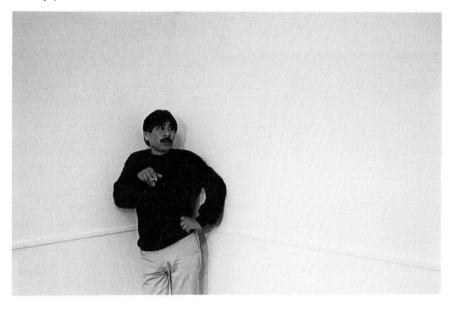

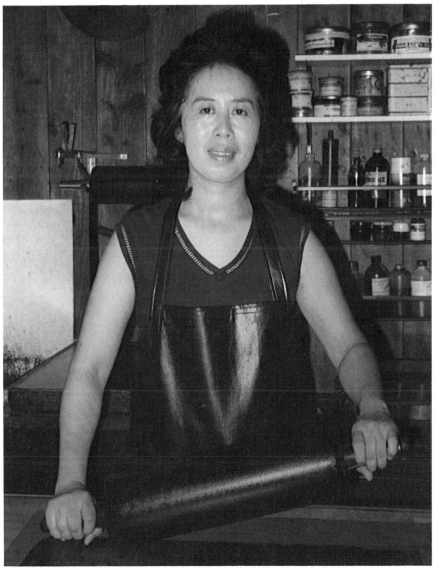

Hoshino Michiko

Hokkaidō, once the most remote part of Japan from its artistic centres but now increasingly productive of good artists as its sense of identity grows stronger. Ikeda was educated at Musashino University of Fine Arts. He has made a considerable reputation with his etchings, based on photography and combined with aquatint and other intaglio processes which add the imaginative dimension. In this approach he partly resembles Noda (no. 45), but unlike him he tries to put the ordinary into an extraordinary context, rather than to encourage it to speak for itself. Here the little Indian girl is completely dwarfed by the massive rock-like structures towering above her, and seems to be rescued only by the artist's comforting 'W' imposed at the top. The print is suffused with a lustrous purple, which gives it a dark energy which appears to come from within.

13 ITŌ Handoku (b.1948)

Uta – 34
1984. 14/20
Woodblock/silkscreen. 510 × 570mm

Itō was born in Shizuoka Prefecture and now lives in Chiba Prefecture. The title also appears written in characters on the print. The meaning of *Uta* is literally 'song', but the word is also used for short Japanese poems, and all the artist's recent prints have used this title with that meaning, followed by a serial number. Itō uses to great effect the contrast of two different techniques. The body of the print is done in woodblock, in black, white and grey, with the grainy texture typical of that medium. Over it bars of shaded silvery grey and black hover mysteriously, their sheen, typical of silkscreen, separating them from the background on which they throw shadows.

14 IWAMI Reika (b.1927)

Reviving Water
1984. Artist's proof (main edition of 70)
Woodblock/embossing. 780 × 525mm

Iwami was born in Tokyo and lives in Kanagawa Prefecture, near the sea, which is featured in most of her prints. She was educated at Bunka University in Tokyo, but her chief influences included the great 'Creative Print' *(Sōsaku Hanga)* pioneer Onchi Kōshirō (1891–1955), his pupil Sekino Jun'ichirō (b.1914), and Shinagawa Takumi (b.1908), from whose collage-like work she has drawn the greatest inspiration. In particular, she has followed Shinagawa's use of pieces of driftwood to print from (an idea which began with Onchi), and her prints always include it. They usually include as well some gold or silver leaf and thick, expressive embossing. This example uses all these to achieve a refined ambiguity – are we

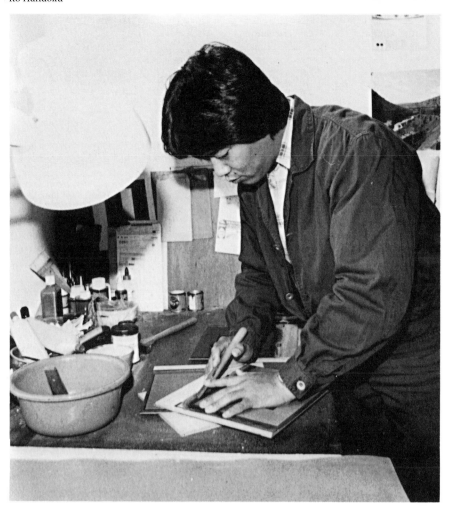

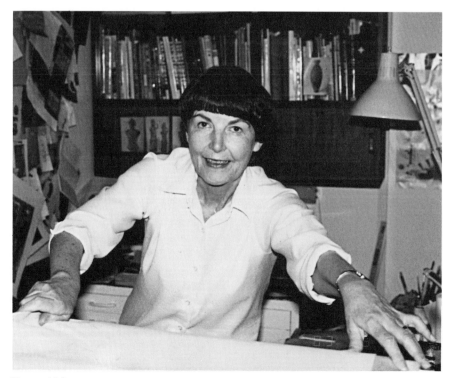

Margaret Johnson

30

looking at water or fire? Iwami is also a *haiku* poet, and the obliqueness of that verse form finds a visual equivalent in her subtle prints.

15 JOHNSON Margaret (b.1918)

Yesterday's Memory
1985. 1/15
Intaglio/embossing. 415 × 545 mm

Margaret Johnson was born in Wisconsin, USA, and now lives in Princeton, New Jersey. Her most important teacher was Josef Albers. She spent the years 1975 to 1983 living and working in Japan, and was inevitably influenced by that experience. Unlike those foreign artists who become entranced with the Japanese scene and wish to record in detail its unique flavour, Johnson has slowly absorbed the quietness, simplicity and tonal subtlety of the Japanese environment and begun to express those feelings in a less direct way. This print, with its grey and buff tonalities, has some of the feeling of a Japanese plaster wall. The central line, deeply scored by embossing, adds to that sense of the physical. Now she has left Japan, the artist's desire to express something of Japanese sensibility seems to be increasing.

16 KAMATANI Shin'ichi (b.1948)

Pinetree No. 37
1985. Artist's proof (main edition of 40)
Silkscreen. 380 × 520 mm

The artist was born in Hyōgo Prefecture and now lives in Yokohama. He was a student at Tokyo University of Fine Arts and still teaches there. He was one of the many pupils of Komai Tetsurō (b.1920) and also learned from Okabe Tokuzō (b.1930). His prints in recent years have all been entitled *Pinetree*, but it is not easy to see the imaginative connection between one of the most ancient subjects of the art of East Asia and these geometrical prints with their obvious debt to Mondrian. As is the case with several prints illustrated in this book, the real source of inspiration seems to be Japanese traditional architecture and interior decoration.

17 KATORI Takeshi (b.1949)

Still Life on the Table I
1983. 30/45
Mezzotint. 215 × 675 mm

It is difficult to imagine, looking at the still-life prints of Katori, that his most important influence was the great woodblock artist Hagiwara Hideo (b.1913), for the master's works have a deliberate roughness of texture which could hardly be more different from the polish and smoothness of Katori. The younger artist uses mezzotint with passionate feeling

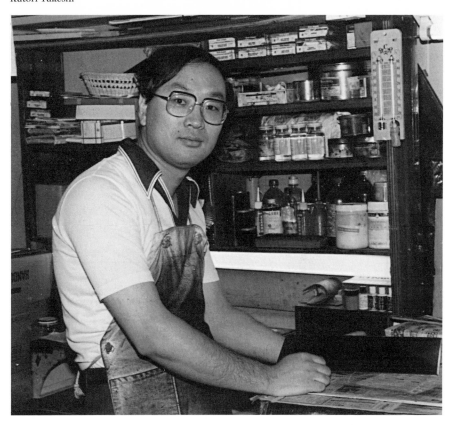

for black and white. At the same time, his subjects are, extraordinarily, still-life assemblages recalling in almost every detail the still-life paintings of seventeenth-century Holland. It is almost as if a modern American artist were trying to reproduce in contemporary graphic technique the *Rimpa* painting of seventeenth-century Japan. As the artistic world becomes ever more wide, interconnected and knowledgeable about other ages and cultures, so will such unexpected, even exotic, creations appear in ever more unexpected circumstances.

18 KAWABE Isshū (b.1941)

Blue Scenery
1985. 2/5
Silkscreen. 500 × 500 mm

The title is translated from the Japanese, in which form it appears on the print. Kawabe was born in Miyazaki Prefecture in Kyūshū, where he still lives, and was educated at Miyazaki University and Saga University of Education. His most important teacher was Saguchi Shichirō. He has said that his objective is to express emotion through colour, and the careful attention he devotes to that colour results in his producing very small editions. This print, indeed, has much more the feeling of a painting, so warmly and sensuously are the tones expressed. The inset girl, suffused with a sun-like golden-orange

light, conveys with direct simplicity the emotional impact of the landscape for the artist.

19 KAWACHI Seikō (b.1948)

'84 Katsura (XII)
1984. Artist's proof (main edition of 98)
Woodblock. 715 × 510 mm

Kawachi was born in Yamanashi Prefecture and studied at Tama University of Fine Arts in Tokyo, in which city he now lives – appropriately, for he is above all the artist of metropolitan stress and tension, phenomena which are very evident in the Japanese capital. But they are familiar to city-dwellers all over the world, and for that reason Kawachi has a truly international appeal. He is the most prominent of the younger artists who have led the revival of the woodblock print as the old *Sōsaku Hanga* movement has lost impetus. His use of the grain and the blemishes of veneer gives vitality to his surfaces. The power of his subject-matter speaks for itself. *Katsura* is a Japanese timber of high quality, and Kawachi's series with this title shows beams of timber cracking under intolerable tension. The sense of sheer scale and massive, uncontrollable forces in these big prints is most remarkable.

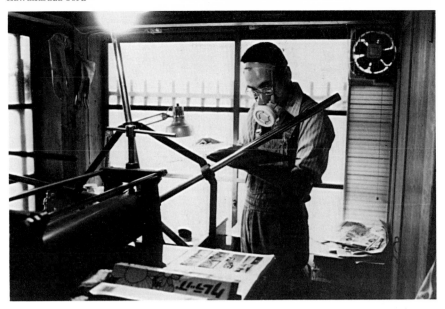

20 KAWAHARADA Tōru (b.1944)

Pumpkin Paradise of the Poor

1983. 15/75
Etching. 400 × 365 mm

Born in Kitakyūshū, Fukuoka Prefecture, where he still lives, Kawaharada was educated at Tokyo University. Of all the artists in this book, he offers the closest approximation to the direct, biting social comment so common in the graphics of Europe and North America. Direct observation of the lower layers of society is not a common subject of 'respectable' art in Japan; mostly it finds expression in the overflowing energy of the country's cartoon culture. Kawaharada, even so, has distanced himself from his subject by using a style of composition more reminiscent of Breughel than of more recent Western models such as German Expressionism. The figures, too, are not specifically Japanese; but the products and activities, most of them labelled, are all available in contemporary Japan – mainly food and drink, but also a stripper, a hairdresser, a sports-shop, and many others. The biggest sign, on the fan projecting above the roof, is *Matsuri* – 'festival'. The title is in Japanese, and refers ironically to the Buddhist 'Pure Land', the 'Paradise' of the English translation.

21 KAWAKUBO Etsuko (b.1960)

Spring

1985. 1/15
Lithograph. 730 × 450 mm

The artist was born in Tokyo and still lives there. Her two most important influences are Arichi Yoshito (no. 2) and Hara Takeshi (no. 9). As one of the youngest artists in this book, she thus names as her teachers men themselves still considered in Japan members of the younger generation. Her work, however, is rather different from the smoothly controlled forms of those artists, and has much more in common with the more eventful surfaces of Margaret Johnson (no. 15) or Norine Nishimura (no. 44). The lithographic medium allows her to express a very direct sense of her personal hand, almost of doodling, on a casually spattered surface which recalls the soil, or perhaps a plaster wall. She also exploits to the full the physical texture of the paper itself.

22 KAWAMURA Jun (b.1926)

New Year

1985. 4/85
Silkscreen. 790 × 460 mm

Kawamura was born in Kōchi Prefecture, one of only two artists in this book from the island of Shikoku (the other is Mori Hidefumi, no. 39). He was trained at the Bunka Gakuin in Tokyo, and still lives in the Japanese capital. His major influence was Shiina Gōmi. Kawamura's most recent work has consisted of carefully worked-out compositions of overlapping bands of primary colours. These are produced by the use of an airbrush onto film, a process which allows the very fine gradations of tone on which these prints depend. The film is then transferred by a light-hardening process to a silkscreen, which can print the effects produced by the airgun with great accuracy.

23 KIDA Yasuhiko (b.1944)

Nebuta Festival I

1984. 5/50
Woodblock. 735 × 355 mm

Kida is a Kyoto-born artist who studied at Kyoto University of Fine Arts and still lives in the ancient capital. He works in the old woodblock technique, with big, energetic designs cut in thick line and large areas of flat black. He sometimes uses a few simple colours, but mostly works in the black and white manner perfected by the great Folk movement artist Munakata Shikō (1903–75). The simplicity and deliberate *naïveté* of his forms and spatial relationships is certainly derived from Japanese folk-style, but it also has a large element of the modern cartoon, which has proved a major sub-culture of Japanese pictorial art. The raw energy of this view of the Nebuta Festival held annually in Aomori Prefecture comes most of all from this source. The huge figures are in fact festival floats, hand-drawn by large numbers of participating men. Kida, in spite of his almost grotesque imagery, is a kindly and affectionate observer of the more traditional activities of Japanese life.

24 KIMURA Hideki (b.1948)

A Waterbird of Mr I

1983. One of an edition of 10 (not numbered on the print)
Silkscreen. 760 × 560 mm

The accomplished smoothness of this interesting print owes much to the artist's teacher at the Kyoto City University of Arts, Yoshihara Hideo (b.1931). But Yoshihara's works are in intaglio or lithograph while Kimura uses silkscreen for his prints, which are usually based on photographs of quite everyday things. Here two superimposed photographs of a man's hands and arms have been cleverly altered and arranged to give the impression of a waterbird and its reflection. The print can be viewed vertically or horizontally, and there is thus a quadruple ambiguity in its composition.

Kimura has remained faithful to the Kansai area of Japan, as he was born in Kyoto and now lives in nearby Shiga Prefecture.

25 KOBAYASHI Jinan (b.1951)

Monument '84-S

1984. 2/30
Etching/mezzotint. 450 × 595 mm

Kobayashi Jinan was born in Ibaragi Prefecture and now lives in Tokyo. He trained at Tōyō Art School in Tokyo, and his work shows great fellow-feeling with that of Hamanishi Katsunori (no. 8). Like Hamanishi, Kobayashi uses the powerful

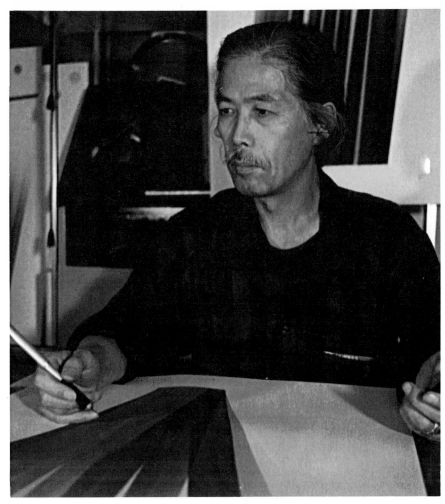

the lithograph artist Ozaku Seishi (b.1936). Her recent prints have been much concerned, according to their titles, with time and memory, but she has also said that they are about the consciousness of city-dwellers, who are now a big majority in Japan as well as in other advanced countries. Born in the remote and very rural prefecture of Niigata, she must be keenly aware of the contrast with the cold regularities of great cities, which are so well represented in her geometrical greys and browns.

28 KURITA Mariko (b.1950)

Scenes and Manners in India – Gaya II
1984. 8/50
Etching. 150 × 415 mm

The title on the print itself is in Japanese only. Kurita was born in Tokyo and now lives in Chiba Prefecture. She names Katō Kiyomi as her most important influence. Her prints on Indian subjects have a strong flavour of their own, detached and sympathetic at the same time. She is not the first Japanese to record the Indian scene, for Yoshida Hiroshi (1876–1950) made many woodblocks of Indian scenes in the 1920s and 1930s, and more recently Ikeda Ryōji (no. 12) has based many of his prints on Indian photographs. But although she uses the old Western etching technique, Kurita is the most traditionally Japanese of the three. This is most noticeable in her choice of an extremely high point of view, which completely obviates the horizon, for this is the pictorial technique of the oldest Japanese paintings on paper and silk, dating back to the eighth century AD.

29 KURODA Shigeki (b.1953)

Purple Haze
1984. 19/50
Etching/aquatint. 295 × 595 mm

Kuroda has been one of the most popular Japanese print artists since the late 1970s, when his compositions based on bicycles and umbrellas first became known among world collectors. Working with various combinations of intaglio processes, sometimes in black and white and sometimes with the addition of colour, he communicates with considerable effect the rush, stress and aimlessness of much modern life. His cyclists, furiously hurrying in one direction, shelter from the world of nature under their umbrellas, which also stop them seeing each other or indeed where they are going. It is a witty image, both satirical and disturbing, which seems to appeal as much in other countries as it does in Japan.

Kuroda was born and still lives in Yokohama, and studied at Tama University of Fine Arts.

contrasts possible in black and white in the mezzotint medium to express his rather disturbing mechanistic fantasies. In this print he exploits the visual contradictions of glass, fabric and stressed metal to produce an image of high tension. Instead of using a velvety black mezzotint background, as in some of his earlier prints, he has etched a brilliantly varied surface which adds even more to the sense of taut expectancy and acts as an effective contrast to the smoothly finished objects in the centre.

26 KOBAYASHI Keisei (b.1944)

In the Silent Time No. 3-A
1984. 6/40
Wood engraving. 205 × 625 mm

The Japanese title, also recorded on the print, may be translated as 'Drifting Ashore: Carving of Resurrection, No. 3-A', an interesting example of the considerable differences which sometimes occur between titles in the two languages. Clearly the Japanese version throws more light on the subject, while the English seems to provide a

different and more mysterious interpretation of this very surrealist print. The artist has used the medium of wood engraving, an unusual one in contemporary Japan, and one which was introduced in the late nineteenth century for the easier reproduction of book illustration. Since the end-grain is used, the blocks are much smaller, and here Kobayashi leaves the joins between his several blocks quite deliberately visible. Wood engraving, like metal intaglio, works from black to white, and proves most suitable for his moonlit erotic nightmare.

Kobayashi was born in Kyoto and studied at the International Art Institute there. He now lives in Tokyo.

27 KOBAYASHI Kiyoko (b.1947)

Continuative Memory
1983. 18/35
Lithograph. 650 × 490 mm

The title appears only in Japanese on the print. Kobayashi was one of the many fine artists trained at Tokyo University of Fine Arts by Komai Tetsurō. She was also influenced by

30 KUROSAKI Akira (b.1937)

Between Moments 1
1984. 28/50
Woodblock. 560 × 820mm

This grand and impressive print could reasonably be described as Kurosaki's finest in the new, darker palette he has adopted since the beginning of the 1980s. As a performance of woodblock-cutting and printing alone it is most remarkable: it has much of the finish one expects from lithograph or silkscreen, but retains the depth of surface and grain of woodblock. The marks of the printer's baren can in fact be seen quite clearly on the dark grey background. With its monumental central shape, seemingly casting a shadow over the middle of the print, its sense of horizontal direction and its drops of water held in potential movement, the whole composition imaginatively lives out its title. The work is also numbered 'W-317' in Kurosaki's continuing print series.

The artist was born in Dalian, Manchuria, and trained at Kyoto Technical University. He still lives in Kyoto.

31 LIAO Shiou-Ping (b.1936)

Rock Garden II
1985. 6/35
Silkscreen/collagraph. 330 × 480mm

Liao was born in Taipei, capital of Taiwan, and after studying at the National Taiwan Normal University and at the Tokyo University of Education, completed his artistic training in France at the Ecole Nationale Supérieure des Beaux-Arts and at Atelier 17 with Stanley Hayter. He now lives in New Jersey, USA, and is thus one of the most international of artists. Yet his imagery is very much of East Asia, both Taiwan and Japan. Here the box, apparently made of paulownia wood, is the traditional type used for valued objects, and contains a rock very reminiscent of those selected for the classical gardens of China. The rock is printed by collagraph, which is a method of building up the surface of a metal plate with resin, glue or similar substances and then printing from it as if from an intaglio plate. The title is also written on the print in Chinese/Japanese characters.

32 MAEDA Morikazu (b.1932)

Bridge on the River
1983. 21/40
Woodblock. 335 × 490mm

Maeda was born in Shizuoka Prefecture, and still lives there. His most influential teacher was the major *Sōsaku Hanga* printmaker Yamaguchi Gen (1903–1976), himself a pupil of the greatest master of that movement, Onchi Kōshirō. His roots naturally, then, lie in that great tradition of woodblock printing, and his most recent works show a very pronounced appreciation of the surface effects produced by that medium. In this example, his bridge seems isolated in the river coruscating in the sunlight. It seems that the true bridge may in fact be the path of light from the sun, running straight towards the viewer. The title of the print also appears in Japanese, and the artist signs his name in Western style, but reversed from right to left.

33 MAKI Haku (b.1924)

Collection 85-10
1985. 5/100
Cement/mortar/woodblock. 135 × 350mm

Maki is sufficiently old-fashioned to sign his prints in characters and to use an old-style seal, carefully placed, as if on a traditional painting. His prints make use of very thick paper, embossed by the use of a cement mould. The subject is a teabowl for the Tea Ceremony. It is of the low-fired pottery known as *Raku*, which since the late sixteenth century has been considered the most suitable for tea ware. Maki achieves an astonishingly real sense of the tactile qualities of *Raku*, which would be readily understood by most

Kuroda Shigeki (no. 29)

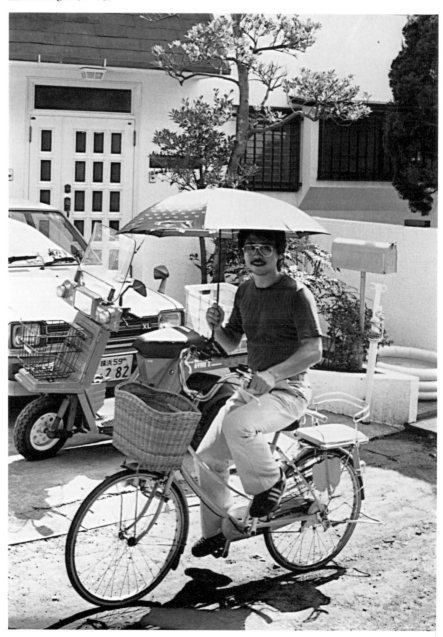

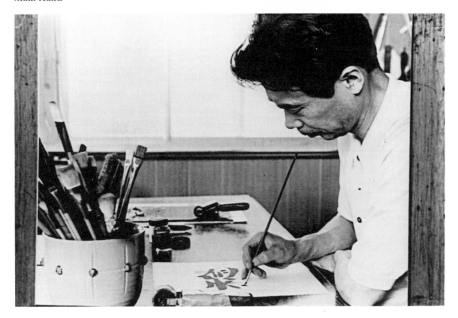

35 MATSUMURA Sei'ichi
(b.1958)

Ground Connection (IV)
1984. Artist's proof (main edition of 10)
Lithograph. 500 × 630 mm

Matsumura was born in Osaka and now lives in Tokyo. His teacher was the lithograph and woodblock artist Ozaku Seishi (b.1936). This print expresses more clearly than any in this book how much the urban world of Japan has in common with the great cities of every country. This bleak scene of concrete and wire could be anywhere, and any time in the last forty years. But the artist adds an element of mystery in the rocks jammed in the wire fence and on the ground. Some of their shapes resemble the flints of prehistoric cultures – the beginnings of the technology which has led to such urban desolation.

36 MATSUSHITA Satoru (b.1957)

Summer Time – 2
1984. 3/15
Woodblock. 600 × 500 mm

This print is especially interesting coming from a young artist, because it is an indication of the gradual swing back to Japan's oldest graphic medium of woodblock among some artists of the youngest generation. The 1960s and 1970s showed a very steady move away from the classic woodblock, but artists like Matsushita are beginning to use it for subjects which only a few years ago would have found a more natural outlet in the technically smoother lithographic or silkscreen techniques. This swimming pool view, in fact, looks at first glance like a lithograph. It shows a clear debt to the work of David Hockney.
Matsushita, a native of Tokyo, studied at the Tokyo University of Fine Arts.

37 MIYOSHI Yukiko (b.1929)

Dice 83-8
1983. 4/20
Silkscreen. 530 × 485 mm

The artist was born and lives in Tokyo, and studied at the Ochanomizu Bunka Gakuin. It has become part of Japan's post-war graphic tradition for some individual artists to pick on an object or aspect of Japanese or universal culture and subject it to repeated variations with very intense scrutiny. The explorations of the visual possibilities of the abacus by Sekine Yoshio (b.1922) are a notable example. Miyoshi here does the same with the variations possible from dice; she comments on the element of chance they represent by superimposing two very certain shapes in red and white. These colours have long been used in Japan to symbolize the conflict of two

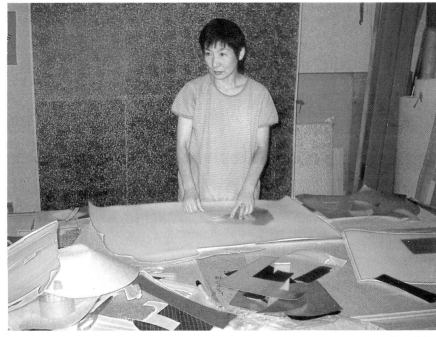

Miyoshi Yukiko

Japanese. The artist was a pupil of the *Sōsaku Hanga* master Onchi Kōshirō and like all his pupils has shown considerable independence of mind. He now lives in Ibaragi Prefecture.

34 MATSUMOTO Akira (b.1936)

Revolve (W5-Negative/Positive)
1985. 4/20
Woodblock. 600 × 600 mm

The title is not written on the print itself. Matsumoto was born in Osaka and now lives

in Tokyo. His master was Mitsumoto Ka'ichi. This print is a most skilful example of woodblock printing and a work of some complexity. It is printed with a series of superimposed blocks in red, grey, blue, yellow and white, each one the result of many hours of cutting. The superimpositions produce the sense of an infinite variety of colours, all revolving, as the title suggests, round the small white central spot which focuses the whole composition. The reverse side of the print is heavily indented, showing the vigorous use of the traditional baren pad to take the impression from the block.

opposites, and Japanese schools normally divide into red and white teams for competitions and sports.

38 MIYOSHI Yuriko (b.1962)

In the Bed
1985. 1/15
Etching/aquatint. 450 × 450 mm

Miyoshi Yuriko is the youngest artist represented in this book. She was born and lives in Chiba Prefecture near Tokyo and was taught by Baba Kashiō (no. 5). From him she has clearly inherited a sense of humour, but her work is of course very much more sombre in its tones than Baba's brilliant palette of primary colours. This reflects the less high-spirited aspect of her work, with its slightly uneasy mixture of surrealist and expressionist elements. At heart this composition is a non-Japanese concept, since in traditional houses it is normal to sleep on the *tatami* mat flooring, and in more modern dwellings one would not see a room or a bed of this old-fashioned type.

39 MORI Hidefumi (b.1953)

Polyphonic Plane 14 (A)
1984. 1/30
Woodblock. 600 × 795 mm

Mori was born in Kagawa Prefecture in the island of Shikoku, and now lives in Tokyo, where he was a student at Tama University of Fine Arts, a school which also produced Kawachi Seikō (no. 19). Kawachi is the leading practitioner of woodblock among the younger generation: the younger Mori has followed in his footsteps by producing prints of great structural force and with surfaces pulsating with the sheer excitement of the medium. He has incorporated into this print, perhaps unconsciously, some of the patterning found in Japanese hand-made papers when the outer fibres are left in the paper-mix; and the overall design recalls to some degree the paper collages produced in earlier periods in Japan as a surface on which to write fine calligraphy. But the title reflects also the great interest in European music which exists in contemporary Japan.

40 MORI Hiroko (b.1942)

Graffiti
1983. 11/50
Etching/aquatint. 360 × 445 mm

Several of the prints illustrated in this book, while appearing at first glance completely international in character, show features that turn out to be very much of East Asian origin. Here, as in nos 28 and 35, the viewpoint of the scene is so high as to be almost overhead.

This is a feature of pictorial construction going back in China to before the Tang Dynasty, which began in the early seventh century AD, and it was never afterwards lost in East Asia. In other respects the scene could be set in many places in the world, though the boys seem to be dressed as contemporary Japanese.

The artist was born and lives in the northern island of Hokkaidō, and studied at the Women's Training College of Art.

41 MORI Yoshitoshi (b.1898)

Shibaraku
1985. 6/70
Stencil. 630 × 410 mm

Like Watanabe Sadao (no. 69), Mori studied stencil-dyeing under Yanagi Sōetsu (1891–1961) and Serizawa Keisuke (1895–1983), but he spent much of his career applying it to textiles; only in the late 1950s did he begin to produce his expansive prints on the subjects of the Kabuki theatre and Japanese festivals and traditional stories. Their simplicity and energy have made him very popular both in his own country and outside it; his work is more collected by foreign galleries than that of any other contemporary Japanese artist. This starkly expressive example, printed in black alone, refers to the famous Kabuki play *Shibaraku* ('Just a Moment') where the hero halts a villainous act with that mighty shout. The actor Danjūrō is shown in the part of the hero, a tribute to the appointment of the twelfth actor of that name in Tokyo in 1985. The artist's red seal is placed, following East Asian tradition, on the composition itself.

42 MURAI Masanari (b.1905)

Square
1985. 16/75
Silkscreen. 480 × 480 mm

Murai was born in Gifu Prefecture, and now lives in Tokyo. He studied at the Bunka Gakuin there, and spent the years 1928–32 in France. His work there gave him confidence in the bold, colourful abstraction then at its height in Europe, and he has remained ever since principally a painter in that style. In more recent years he has designed prints as a subsidiary activity – a practice more usual among Western artists than Japanese – and has been content to have them printed in any medium which will do justice to his compositions. In spite of this visual abstraction, Masanari's interests are mainly psychological, and in this print he has vividly portrayed his view of a solid personality through the massive certainties of his blocks and wedges of black on a confident red ground.

43 NAKABAYASHI Tadayoshi (b.1937)

Transposition '83 – Ground – 1
1983. Artist's proof (main edition of 50)
Etching/aquatint. 565 × 485 mm

Nakabayashi, who is Professor of the Print Department at Tokyo University of Fine Arts, studied there under Komai Tetsurō and has passed on his skills in the intaglio processes to a new generation, including artists such as Umezawa Kazuo (no. 67). Over the last quarter-century his prints have explored in ever greater depth the possibilities of black and white, and it is fair to claim that his most recent works have reached a new level of complexity and emotional expressiveness. The densely worked surface of the print illustrated here is made up of a combination of natural plants and grasses with abstract shapes, dependent in no small measure for their effect on the thick Kōchi paper specially ordered by the artist. Nakabayashi's technique is too complicated to describe in a book of this length, but the result is intensely individual.

44 NISHIMURA Norine (b.1952)

Easter Sunday, La Califusa, 1984
1984. 5/20
Woodblock/*chine collé*. 775 × 550 mm

One of several non-Japanese artists who have lived and worked in Japan for significant parts of their artistic lives, Norine Nishimura is an American born in Chicago and now living in California. Like some other prominent foreign printmakers, she learned Japanese techniques under the woodblock artist Kurosaki (no. 30), but her work could scarcely be further removed from his brilliantly coloured style, being more closely influenced by the more restrained side of the Japanese environment, even when the subject is American. In the traditional European *chine collé* technique, a very thin sheet of paper takes up the impression from the printing plate, and is in the same operation laminated by a special adhesive onto a thicker backing paper. Nishimura varies this by applying pieces of thinner paper to parts of her printing surface by hand. The effects produced depend on whether this is done before or after the main printing.

45 NODA Tetsuya (b.1940)

Diary: April 23rd '83, in Kyoto
1983. 12/20
Woodblock/silkscreen. 670 × 460 mm

In the early 1970s Noda found a uniquely personal technique for expressing the events in his life – internal or external – and has kept to it ever since, dazzling the international print world with his seemingly endless variety and capacity for change and development. The technique consists of taking a black and white photograph, altering the plate, passing it through a mimeograph machine to produce a screen of dots, and printing through a silkscreen. The background has already been filled in with woodblock, usually in white to contrast with the buff of the Japanese paper. Recently Noda has turned to townscape and landscape. Here a willow tree on a motorway in Kyoto stands like a monument to the ink-painting traditions of East Asia, poignantly isolated in a hostile urban environment. The fact that the motorway is in Kyoto, Japan's ancient artistic capital, adds an unbearable irony to the point.

Noda was trained at the Tokyo University of Fine Arts, where he still teaches as a colleague of Nakabayashi (no. 43).

46 ONO Tadashige (b.1909)

Flying
1971. Edition of 50 (this print not numbered)
Woodblock. 140 × 217 mm

Ono Tadashige is one of the grand old men of the 'Creative Print' movement (*Sōsaku Hanga*), having been a major advocate of proletarian art in the 1930s. His work is much concerned with ordinary townscapes and unpretentious landscape, to all of which he adds the special glow of his rich oil-based pigments. This is the only work in this book originated before 1982, but in spite of its comparatively early date of 1971 it was only recently printed, as Ono has almost stopped producing new designs. This practice of taking pulls from older blocks is common among the older-style woodblock artists, who often only slowly fill up an edition over the years. The title, in both languages, is on a slip attached to the back of the print.

Ono was educated at the Hongo Art Institute, and now lives in Tokyo.

47 ŌNUMA Masaaki (b.1953)

Concerto – M-II
1985. 1/20
Etching/aquatint/mezzotint. 580 × 420 mm

The title is translated from the Japanese. Ōnuma was born in Yamagata Prefecture, and now lives in Kanagawa Prefecture to the south-west of Tokyo. He was a pupil of the powerful colour-intaglio artist Horii Hideo (b.1934), from whom he has adopted an interest in including mysterious female figures in his prints. This work, however, should not be treated as a solemn one. It is more of a visual witticism. The most prominent newspaper section, printed by photo-engraving, mentions 'France's Fading Reds', which are neatly commented on by the scattered roses. The newspaper excerpts are all taken from Japan's English-language dailies, which seem to be preferred as pictorial material by contemporary artists because of their more international flavour.

48 ŌYAMA Emiko (b.1958)

Scenery Unremembered
1984. 5/20
Etching. 550 × 785 mm

The artist was born in Gumma Prefecture and now lives, like so many printmakers, in Tokyo. She was a student at Sōkei Art School. The title of the print is translated from the Japanese. It is not at all clear where this scene is set, and whether the buildings are farm or factory. The presence of a sheep, not at all a common animal in Japan, printed in an olive-grey inset, adds to the enigma; so do the slashing horizontal and vertical lines. As is so often the case among young printmakers in Japan, the apparently international nature of the work has underlying traditional attitudes, especially in black and white works, which almost inevitably reflect the calligraphic tradition in brush and black ink and the related history of ink painting in the Far East.

49 PETIT Gaston (b.1930)

Invitatoire
1984. 17/55
Silkscreen. 590 × 450 mm

Gaston Petit was born in Canada and educated at the Dominican House of Studies in Ottawa. For many years he has lived in Tokyo and worked as one of the most original and varied printmakers in that city. In this sardonically humorous work he has put together visual elements from Japanese tradition and surrounded them with the Korean *hangul* script in a dark grid marked 'Boin' (vowels) and 'Shiin' (consonants). The mask represents Okame, the comic goddess of Shintō; around her are the dried *hōzuki* fruits beloved by Japanese children; and at the bottom are reproductions of popular prints of courtesans by Utamaro (1753–1806), on the right, and Eishō (early nineteenth century). Only the paper bag into which Okame has been dropped reminds us that this is contemporary Japan.

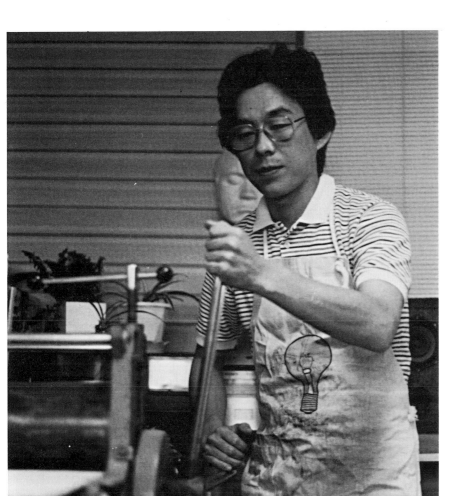

Ōnuma Masaaki

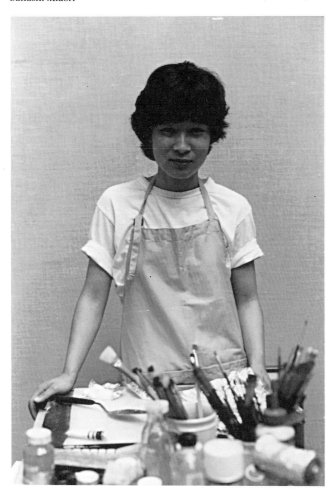 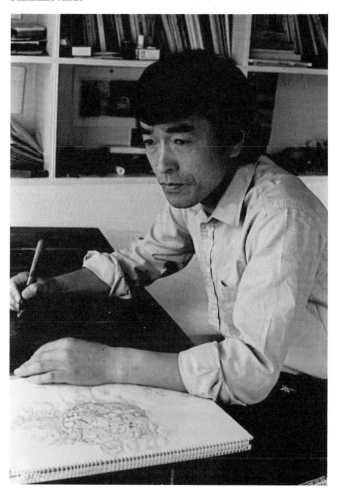

50 SAHASHI Midori (b.1954)

Water in Water No. 9
1984. 3/20
Etching. 365 × 365 mm

This is the quietest, most restrained and perhaps the most Japanese of all the prints reproduced in this book, relying for its effect on its texture and extreme subtlety of tone. At first glance, it looks like a paper collage, but it is in fact an etching of great delicacy, in two tones of pale cream, the outer one edged with the softest of ink lines and washes. The tonalities recall the fine distinctions between Japanese hand-made papers, ranging from near-white to deep beige, colours found in the papers on sliding doors, the backs of folding screens, and in the woven *tatami* mats of traditional flooring.

The artist was born in Nagoya and still lives in Aichi Prefecture. Her teacher was Nomura Hiroshi.

51 SAITŌ Kaoru (b.1931)

Red Illusion Series – Swallowtails
1983. Artist's proof (main edition of 85)
Mezzotint/aquatint. 365 × 300 mm

Saitō Kaoru lives in Kanagawa Prefecture, where he was born. He is basically self-taught in the difficult mezzotint medium, and he names as the most influential artists on him the Western-style painters Tsuruta Gorō and Arai Tatsuo. Together with the European-trained Hamaguchi Yōzō (b.1909), he is the most accomplished technician in mezzotint working in Japan today, and his prints have a finish and perfection which it would be difficult to equal. His studies of women combine a traditional Japanese aesthetic with an almost Pre-Raphaelite romanticism. The subject of this example displays the back of her neck in the manner most admired in the *Ukiyoe* prints of the eighteenth and nineteenth centuries, and has the make-up of a court lady of still earlier ages, but her earrings are of course a twentieth-century feature. The title appears on the print in Japanese as well as in English.

52 SAITŌ Takeshi (b.1943)

Memory – 85-III
1985. 3/30
Etching/aquatint. 450 × 560 mm

Saitō studied at the Musashino University of Fine Arts near Tokyo. He was born in Yamanashi Prefecture, where he still lives. Many of his recent prints have placed simple plants such as cacti or asparagus on a background designed to recall the world of technology – for example, squared paper. This latest work takes the rather grander subject of the 3rd millennium BC stone circle of Stonehenge in England and miniaturizes it against similar material, including a surveyor's pole. It is an apt comment on the technological nature and skill of even such an ancient and revered monument. The artist has kept to his favoured palette, which is dominated by orange, yellow and black.

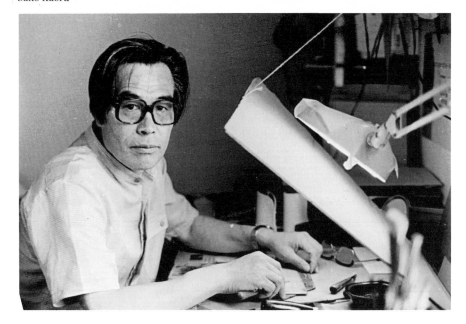

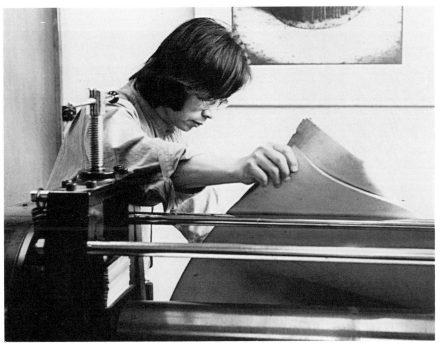

Saitō Takeshi

53 SAKAZUME Atsuo (b.1941)

Safari Land – Empty Heart
1984. 15/20
Mezzotint. 590 × 690 mm

The artist was born in Gumma Prefecture, studied at Kyoto University, and now lives in Kyoto. Some years ago, Sakazume's mezzotints made full use of the dark effects possible in that medium to design prints full of contorted bodies helpless in black space. More recently he has hit on the jigsaw motif to represent that sense of dislocation which he

feels in common with so many modern printmakers. This print loses none of its pathos for being also light-hearted and visually witty. The title is translated from the Japanese which appears on the print, and may be an oblique reference to the Buddhist doctrine of emptiness which would be familiar to every educated Japanese.

54 SAKUMA Yoshiaki (b.1947)

Landscape 84-05
1984. 4/20
Etching/aquatint. 360 × 550 mm

Sakuma was born in Aichi Prefecture and trained at the Kyoto Metropolitan University of Arts. He still lives in the ancient capital of Kyoto. His work follows some of the same themes as that of Saitō Takeshi (no. 52), themes which are common preoccupations in advanced urban civilizations throughout the world. The image of the box – unnatural, man-made, restricting – is increasingly common in the work of artists of that environment. Sakuma shares with Saitō Takeshi (no. 52) the symbol of the surveyor's pole, always a warning that the natural world is about to be further disturbed. There is in this print a strong atmosphere of urban loneliness, surrounded by a landscape resembling a desert without horizons.

55 SAWADA Tetsurō (b.1935)

Brilliant Scape (Blue)
1985. 77/120
Silkscreen. 580 × 400 mm

The title is not on the print itself. The skyscapes of Sawada have become known and admired in many countries of the world, for their appeal seems to be universal and their brilliantly polished silkscreen technique fits contemporary ideals of interior design. Sawada was born in Hokkaidō, where the clearer northern skies, especially in winter, must have provided the first origins of his subject-matter. Since becoming a successful international artist, he has had continuing opportunities to observe the sky in all its moods from the aircraft which he travels in so often to exhibitions around the world. In his explorations of the sky, Sawada has moved far from the artistic traditions of East Asia, where until the late nineteenth century it was usual to express the sky in paintings by simply leaving the paper or silk blank.

The artist studied at Musashino University of Fine Arts and now lives in Tokyo.

56 SHIMIZU Momo (b.1944)

Lines No. 104
1983. 3/10
Silkscreen. 600 × 800 mm

Shimizu was born in Gifu Prefecture and educated at Gifu Prefectural Gunjō High School. He now lives in Tokyo. In this print he has used the very strong horizontal textures of his paper and played them against the vertical movement of his design. The immediate mood of this highly polished silkscreen is that of modern theatrical lighting techniques, with colours mysteriously shifting into each other. The colours used, however, have much in common with the traditional palette of Japanese textile dyeing, especially in the medieval period, and also with the paper-collage surfaces of the same era. These influences may not be conscious, but they cannot be dismissed in a country with such a general awareness of its cultural past.

57 SHINKAI Fumiko (b.1952)

'85-X
1985. 1/10
Etching/drypoint. 485 × 695 mm

Shinkai was born in Aichi Prefecture, and lives in Nagoya, its biggest city. She was a student at the Nagoya College of Design. This print, like no. 58, is best interpreted in the light of the ancient East Asian tradition of calligraphy with brush and ink. The twelve lines which alone make up the entire composition would naturally be looked at as brush-strokes by a Japanese viewer used to the more avant-garde styles of calligraphy. The texturing possible with the drypoint technique enables the artist to print the contrast between the wet and dry edges of a brush-stroke. On the actual print, the lines also produce the illusion of crumpled paper.

58 SHINOHARA Takeshi (b.1951)

And Human and – Rain 2
1985. 1/10
Silkscreen. 800 × 700 mm

Although this austere print is done by silkscreen, it is nevertheless as much related to the East Asian calligraphic tradition as no. 57, with some of the wild dislocation found in the calligraphy of Zen priests and the same careful calculation of the blank spaces. The artist gives some clues in his little typewritten text to what the print is really about, and the reference to the great active volcano of Mt Asama is enough to guide the imagination.

Shinohara was born in the ancient capital of Kyoto, and studied at the Osaka University of Fine Arts. He still lives in Osaka, which is no longer the important centre of graphic art it was until the early nineteenth century.

59 SHIROKI Toshiyuki (b.1938)

Transformation – XI
1984. 2/50
Mezzotint. 600 × 450 mm

Shiroki was born in Nagano Prefecture. He was trained at Tokyo University of Education and now lives in Ibaragi Prefecture. In recent years his intaglio prints have concentrated on the subject of melting steel bars, blocks and tubes, reproduced with a fierce incandescence which seems to grow naturally out of the

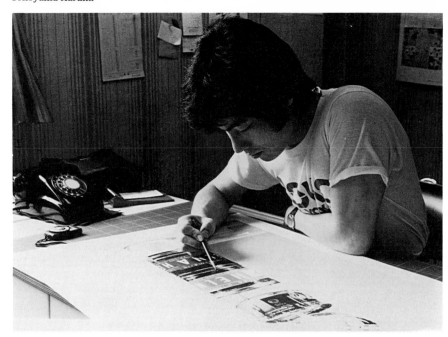

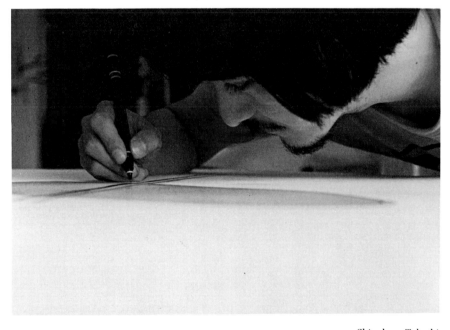

Shinohara Takeshi

black and white contrasts of the mezzotint process. Shiroki's prints at their best have a monumental, almost architectural, scale which can only be paralleled among modern Japanese print artists in the woodblock works of Kawachi Seikō (no. 19) and Morozumi Osamu (b.1949). There is in these artists a feeling of brutally great forces which overwhelm and exclude the merely human.

60 SONOYAMA Harumi (b.1950)

D'encres – O
1985. 6/30
Lithograph. 780 × 540 mm

Born in Kitakyūshū in Fukuoka Prefecture, Sonoyama now lives in Tokyo. He was one of the many lively print artists to be trained at the Tokyo University of Fine Arts. Using the artistic and technical vocabulary of Pop Art, of which his work is a late development, he has made the subject of his more recent lithographs the very inks (produced in France) employed to print them. In a sense,

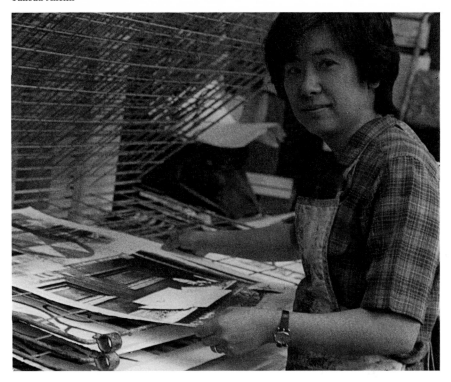

Takeda Akemi

then, these are works of art about art itself. In spite of the apparent gaudiness of his big, cheery lithographs, Sonoyama has a very fine sense of colour, and in the example illustrated has made an impressive composition based on red, black and grey, with a surprisingly strong impact when seen in full size.

61 SUDA Toshio (b.1931)

Midnight Sun I
1985. 6/50
Etching. 450 × 600 mm

Suda was born in Nagoya in Aichi Prefecture and still lives there. His most important influence is Satō Nobuo (b.1926), an artist who has produced colour mezzotints of cherries and shells a little in the manner of the master Hamaguchi Yōzō. He therefore falls within the main line of the intaglio tradition in Japan, and uses etching with an imaginative verve typical of contemporary Japanese graphics. His recent works have used the very unusual motif of disintegrating birds' feathers to express a sense of uneasy bewilderment, a frame of mind relatively common among the Japanese artists of today. The title is translated from the Japanese supplied by the artist.

62 TAKAHASHI Rikio (b.1917)

Niwa (Movement B2)
1985. 7/50
Woodblock. 820 × 545 mm

Takahashi is one of the last masters of the 'Creative Print' movement *(Sōsaku Hanga)*. In his youth he was one of the last associates of Onchi Kōshirō (d.1955) and has explored with persistent intensity the semi-abstract woodblock style perfected by the master in the last ten years of his life. Takahashi shows in this print the main features of that style – quiet but warm and very harmonious colours, much use of space, the overlapping of blocks of colour to produce interesting nuances of tone, and the use of almost recognizable pictorial elements such as rocks. The artist, who now lives in Atami in Shizuoka Prefecture, continues to use the theme of the Japanese garden *(Niwa)* seen from above as the basis for his dignified and poetic works.

63 TAKEDA Akemi (b.1951)

Fallout Shelter
1985. Artist's proof (main edition of 25)
Silkscreen. 740 × 505 mm

The title, in English only, is on the back of the print. The artist was born in Kanagawa Prefecture and was educated at Wakō University and at the Pratt Institute in New York. Her residence is now in New York, and

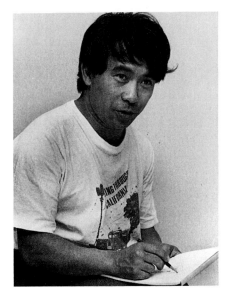

Takeda Hideo

she has thus placed herself at the heart of one of the great innovative centres of contemporary graphics. This print is in the American tradition of social comment and criticism which has been so strong since the 1920s but which has never been a major part of native Japanese art because of the censorship practised by successive governments until 1952. Since then, social comment has remained oblique in Japanese art: direct use of unpalatable photographs such as this as a basis for vivid silkscreen compositions is most unusual within the native Japanese scene.

64 TAKEDA Hideo (b.1948)

Mark of the Fan
1985. 127/185
Silkscreen. 395 × 530 mm

This is one of the *Gempei* series designed by Takeda to mark the 800th anniversary of the Battle of Dan-no-Ura, the climax of the great civil wars between the Minamoto and Taira families. These wars have been celebrated in literature and art ever since. Takeda has chosen a style which is close enough to the heroic woodblock prints of Utagawa Kuniyoshi (1797–1861) to satirize them, yet laced with a fantastic eroticism which is mainly absent from those prints but which Takeda implies is present in the way contemporary Japanese look at them. The story so irreverently treated is that of Munataka. He shot from his horse at a fan placed on the mast of a Taira ship by a Taira noblewoman, risking disgrace if he missed. Takeda has placed a naked woman on the mast as well, and filled the sea with shapes suggesting female bodies.

The artist was born in Osaka and lives in Tokyo. He was educated at Tama University of Fine Arts, a school with adventurous traditions.

65 TANABE Kazurō (b.1937)

Distance B-V
1984. 6/10
Silkscreen. 400 × 520 mm

Tanabe comes from Yokohama and now lives

Tomihari Hiroshi

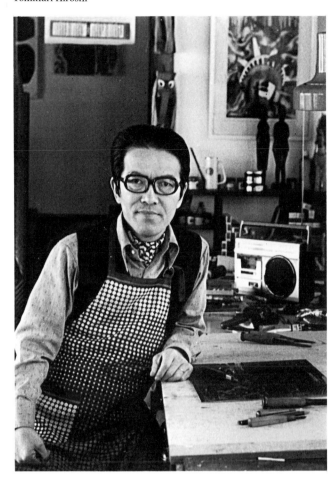

Watanabe Sadao

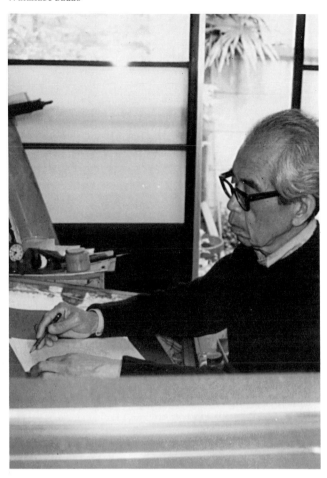

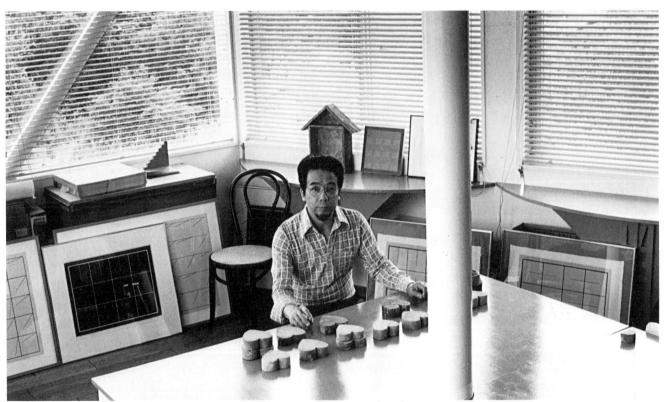

Tanabe Kazurō

in Tokyo. He was trained at Tōhoku University in Sendai, northern Japan, and also spent some time at the London studio of Birgit Skjöld (d.1983), where a number of Japanese graphic artists worked, including Hara Takeshi (no. 9). Most of Tanabe's recent prints have been apparently simple groupings on a grid pattern of outline shapes on a flat background. This example reduces his shapes to even greater simplicity. He prints in black alone, leaving lines in the natural colour of the paper. It is possible to interpret this print as a move towards minimalism, or, more probably, as a return to that extreme simplification of form which is always implied in Japanese traditional architecture and interior design.

66 TOMIHARI Hiroshi (b.1936)

In Praise of Torsos – O
1985. 3/50
Woodblock. 570 × 765 mm

Tomihari was born in Ibaragi Prefecture, educated at Ibaragi University and now lives in Saitama Prefecture. He was one of the early leaders of the revival of woodblock which has been an interesting and encouraging feature of Japanese graphics in recent years. Tomihari has found new expressive power in the medium, using a black and white dotted technique to build up surging vortices of straight and curved shapes. His range of subjects is large, but here the theme is the human body celebrated with force and passion. His sculptural interests are very clear in his prints, and in this he has been followed by the younger Morozumi Osamu and Mori Hidefumi (no. 39).

67 UMEZAWA Kazuo (b.1952)

The Level of the Water – 14
1983. 8/55
Mezzotint. 360 × 300 mm

Umezawa was born in Hokkaidō, and now lives in Saitama Prefecture near Tokyo. His most important teachers were the etchers Komai Tetsurō and Nakabayashi Tadayoshi (no. 43), and it is to the latter, head of the Print Department at Tokyo University of Fine Arts, that he evidently owes the most. He shares with Nakabayashi an interest in the depths which can be explored in black and white intaglio prints, but it is necessary to stress that these depths come in the end from the great East Asian tradition of ink painting. This mezzotint bears more than an accidental resemblance to the many ink paintings of pine trees found in that tradition, in spite of the title, which Umezawa uses for all his prints. However, the artist has extended the tonal range by the use of beige rather than white at the bottom of the print.

68 WAKO Syūji (b.1953)

Still Life, Blue
1985. Artist's proof (main edition of 30)
Lithograph. 825 × 600 mm

Wako was born in Sendai in northern Honshū and educated at Tokyo University of Fine Arts. His most important teachers were Baba Kashiō (no. 5) and Hara Takeshi (no. 9). From the former he has clearly inherited a tendency to light-hearted fantasy, and from the latter a smooth and even elegant use of the lithographic medium. His brilliantly coloured prints often feature objects from the traditional culture of Japan, but arranged so as to seem contemporary. In this print he uses as his main focus an object resembling a celestial globe, which has a somewhat modern appearance although the first ones were introduced into Japan in the seventeenth century. More obviously traditional is the blue fabric decorated with fan shapes.

69 WATANABE Sadao (b.1913)

Last Supper '85
1985. 5/100
Stencil. 620 × 710 mm

Watanabe lists as his teachers two of the great founders of the Japanese Folk Art movement, Yanagi Sōetsu and Serizawa Keisuke, and his prints never deviate from their ideal of honesty to traditional techniques and materials. He has particularly followed Serizawa in his graphic use of the stencil technique, producing images of that monumental simplicity also found in the work of Mori Yoshitoshi (no. 41), who studied under the same masters. Watanabe also prints on hand-crumpled paper, traditionally used for book-covers and end-papers, and this gives his works an almost three-dimensional feeling when held in the hands. His palette is limited to a few rich, natural pigments. Although his prints are always on Christian subjects, their technique is entirely Japanese, and even their figural style is very close to the popular Buddhist prints of earlier periods.

70 WATANABE Toyoshige (b.1931)

A Circle, a Square, a Triangle, a Stick and a Point
1984. 6/30
Silkscreen. 430 × 640 mm

The title is translated from the Japanese which appears on the print. There is also a subtitle, 'Picnic No. 8404'. Watanabe was born in Tokyo and now lives in Kanagawa Prefecture. His most important teacher was Nambata Tatsuoki. This cheerful print is perhaps closer to painting than to printmaking: such closeness to the finish of

Watanabe Toyoshige

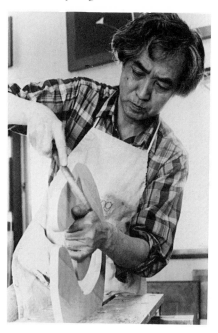

easel painting is especially well achieved with the silkscreen process, which also provides that strength of brilliant colour which is difficult to effect with woodblock or intaglio. The Japanese artist's natural sense of balance is well used in this juggling act of contradictory shapes.

71 YAGAMI Kazutoshi (b.1942)

Works 42-E
1984. 3/20
Silkscreen. 520 × 730 mm

Yagami was born and still lives in Aichi Prefecture, and was educated at Aichi Technological High School. His work shows considerable independence, as might be expected away from the mainstreams of graphic art in Tokyo and Kyoto. In this compelling and forceful print, he uses the smoothness of the silkscreen medium to express the clean lines and careful presentation of contemporary galleries for paintings, prints and sculpture. This is a scene familiar to almost every artist, but instead of works of art the viewer is presented with mirrors reflecting himself. It is not too fanciful to suggest that this is an artist's oblique comment on all who look at works of art and criticize them, as well as a comment on the nature of art itself.

72 YAMANAKA Gen (b.1954)

Looking at the Stars I
1983. 16/30
Woodblock. 500 × 355 mm

The title appears on the print only in Japanese, and literally means 'A man looking at the stars'. The artist is much preoccupied with restricted views through windows and doors, usually onto a black and mysterious starry sky and usually with a white monolith much in evidence. Surrealist imagery of this sort has tended to be expressed in intaglio or silkscreen techniques, but Yamanaka has decided to use the more traditional woodblock for his works, with no loss of the clarity necessary for such effects.

Yamanaka was born in Fukushima Prefecture and trained at Tokyo University of Fine Arts, the cradle of so many imaginative young print artists. He lives in Saitama Prefecture.

73 YAMANOBE Yoshio (b.1936)

Crystal Board I
1985. E.P. (main edition of 30)
Mezzotint. 530 × 790 mm

Yamanobe was born in Fukushima Prefecture and now lives in Tokyo. Like many intaglio artists, he was taught and influenced by the pioneer Komai Tetsurō, and has in turn passed on his skills to others, among them Hamanishi Katsunori (no. 8). This print makes full use of the sinister effects which can be produced using the basically black base of mezzotint. It is a mixture of surrealism with still life, combining familiar objects with the unrecognizable. The sense of unease, so common in contemporary Japanese art, is very evident. In spite of its apparently international flavour, this print features prominently a trailing gourd, which is one of the commonest elements of traditional Japanese decorative art.

74 YAYANAGI Gō (b.1933)

Man and Universe No. 3
1983. 43/50
Silkscreen. 690 × 485 mm

Yayanagi was born in the northern island of Hokkaidō and was educated at Hoshi Pharmaceutical College before learning his craft from Stanley Hayter in Paris, where many Japanese have absorbed the international scene. Since the mid-1960s, when he became one of the leading Japanese advocates of Pop Art, Yayanagi has remained faithful to his cheerful, witty and detached style, which records with gusto and in brilliantly finished colours the passing fads and enthusiasms of the contemporary high-technology world. In the eighteenth or nineteenth centuries he would perhaps have been an *Ukiyoe* artist, recording with delighted abandon the novelties of the urban world of courtesans, actors, fashion and wrestlers.

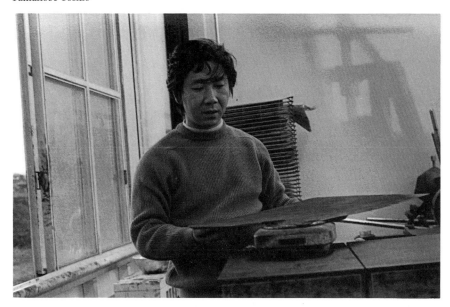

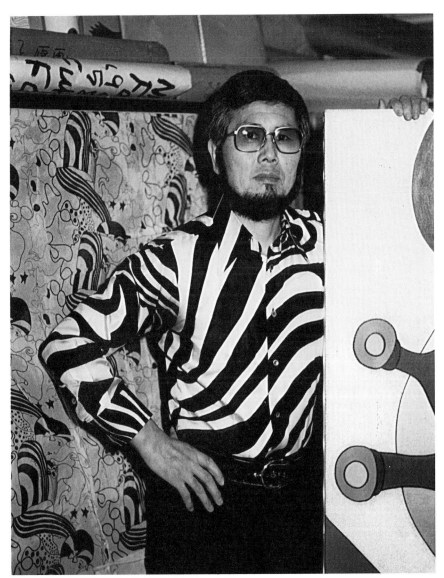

Yayanagi Gō

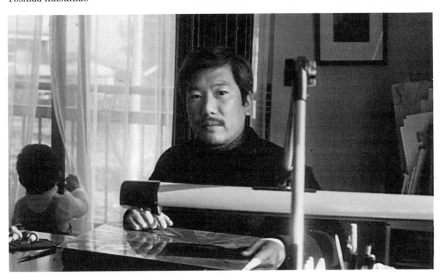

75 YOSHIDA Ayomi (b.1958)

Linear Composition L27-MBP
1984. 10/20
Woodblock. 600 × 600mm

The youngest member of the Yoshida printmaking family, daughter of Yoshida Hodaka and Chizuko (nos 77 and 76), Ayomi has taken up with renewed fervour the use of pure woodblock in the traditional technique, impressed strongly from the back with the baren rubbing-pad. This gives her prints a vibrant, living surface, while their backs have almost as much visual appeal owing to the vigour of the artist's wrists. For this reason, her works come out in small editions. She is interested in the particularly warm colour effects which can be achieved by the superimposition of different carved blocks, and the print illustrated glows almost like a stained-glass window.

The artist was born and resides in Tokyo, and was trained at Wakō University.

76 YOSHIDA Chizuko (b.1924)

Season B
1985. 15/75
Woodblock/etching. 590 × 590mm

The artist is a member of the printmaking family founded by Yoshida Hiroshi (1876–1950), having married his son Hodaka (no. 77). She was born in Yokohama, and now lives in Tokyo. Educated at a girls' art high school, she has nevertheless been most influenced by the woodblock techniques of the Yoshida family. However, like her husband, she has recently varied her textures by the addition of engraving, in this case used on the purple background. Her passionate interest in butterflies and close study of them gives her prints, which are almost always based on them, a surprising intensity. In this she follows, perhaps unconsciously, in a long tradition of Japanese art where strong emotion is suggested in compositions which are on the surface no more than decorative. The paintings of Itō Jakuchū (1716–1800) are her most obvious Japanese predecessors in this manner.

77 YOSHIDA Hodaka (b.1926)

Green Mud Wall
1983. 25/50
Woodblock/etching. 680 × 510mm

The full title of this print is in Japanese and can be translated 'From My Collection – Green Mud Wall'. Yoshida was born in Tokyo, where he still lives, and was educated at Daiichi High School. Far more significantly, he is the younger son of Yoshida Hiroshi, the celebrated print landscapist, whose woodblock style and technique was clearly the most important early influence on him. From the 1950s, however, he developed an individual abstract style, and in the late 1970s began to become interested in photo-etching, with a consequent change to more representational subjects. More recently he has successfully combined both, as in this example, where the background is in woodblock, producing a softer and less starkly analytical view of one of Japan's traditional walls in mud-plaster over straw.

78 YOSHIDA Katsuhiko (b.1947)

F-Pier at Shinkaichi – Before the Evening Shower
1984. 39/50
Mezzotint. 115 × 360mm

The title appears on the print only in its Japanese version. Shinkaichi is part of Kōbe, the great seaport to the west of Ōsaka, considered since the late nineteenth century one of the 'exotic' places of Japan because of its strong international links. Yoshida has chosen an appropriately foreign style, very reminiscent of American pre-war cityscape prints and their post-war derivatives, such as the early work of Hamaguchi Yōzō. The style has recently enjoyed a revival in the USA, and Yoshida is probably responding to that trend.

Yoshida was born in Tokyo and lives in Ibaragi Prefecture. He studied oil painting at Tama University of Fine Arts, but his master in graphics was the intaglio printmaker Komai Tetsurō.

79 ZHANG Yuan Fan (b.1952)

Travelogue (I)
1985. 3/50
Woodblock. 250 × 390mm

Zhang was born in China, but he received his artistic education at the Tokyo University of Fine Arts and now lives in Chiba Prefecture. The title of the print is given in Japanese – Yūki (I). This sober print combines two traditions. One is that of serious abstraction pioneered by Onchi Kōshirō, inspired by European models, a style which is still producing good work in Japanese graphics. The other is the East Asian and originally Chinese tradition of ink painting, which has had a powerful influence on a number of print artists who have been tempted to express in woodblock, etching, mezzotint or lithograph the subtleties possible with brush and ink. Zhang thus combines strands from Europe, China and Japan into his cool and precise style.

80 ZWANG Adriana (b.1946)

Mountains View
1982. 5/20
Woodblock, photo-engraving. 440 × 600mm

This print, like much of the artist's work, reflects her international background. Adriana Zwang was born in Buenos Aires of Argentinian parents. Her artistic education took place first at Bezalel University in Israel and later at Tama University of Fine Arts in Tokyo, where her most important teacher was Fukita Fumiaki (b.1926), a woodblock artist well known for his brilliant prints exploring the effects of radiant light. This work shows a strong preoccupation with contemporary issues, brought out by the newspaper extracts on the world economy and on the Falklands War of 1982. These are transferred by the photo-engraving process, while the remainder of the print is in woodblock. The message at the top, acting as a subtitle to the print, is 'The Nature of the Country is Changing'. This sense of transience and of profound unease permeates much of the artist's work, as it does the work of many other international printmakers today.

The Plates

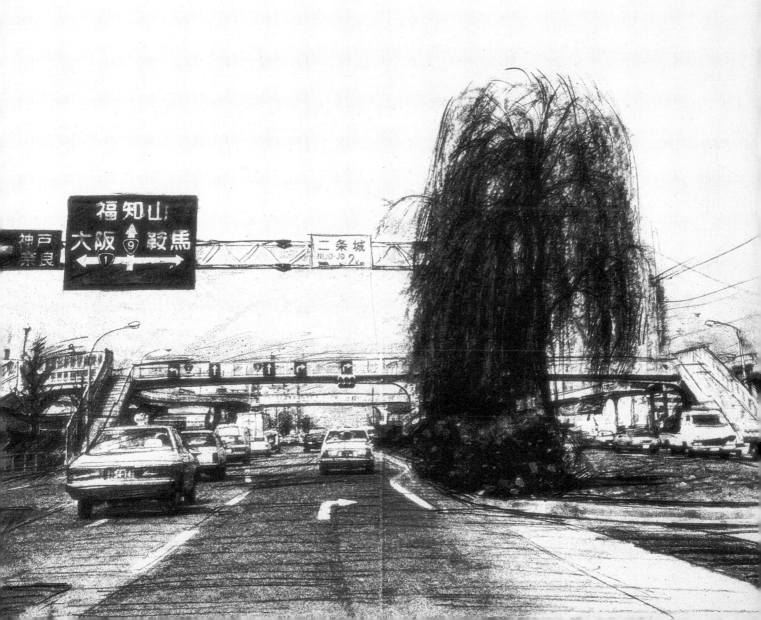

1 AMANO Junji: *Edge 85-K-9*. Silkscreen/embossing, 570 × 845 mm

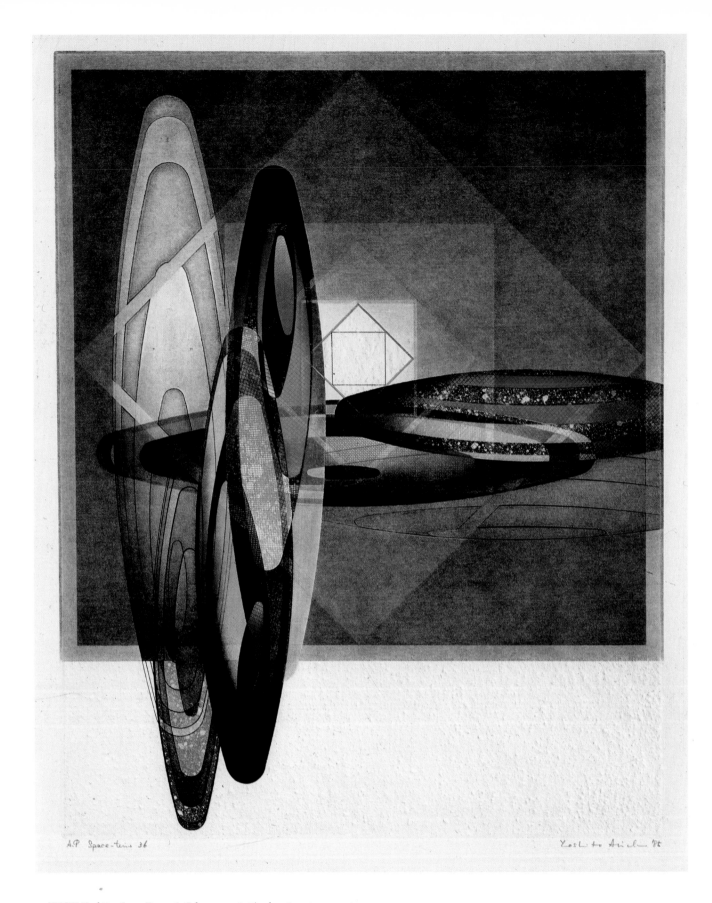

2 ARICHI Yoshito: *Space-Time 36*. Colour aquatint/embossing, 510 × 405 mm

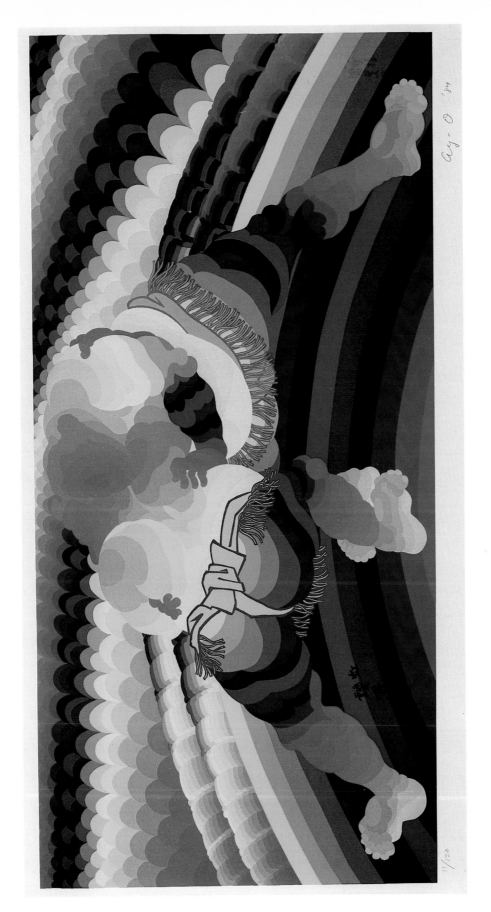

3 AY-Ō: *Sumō Wrestling*. Silkscreen, 400 × 825 mm

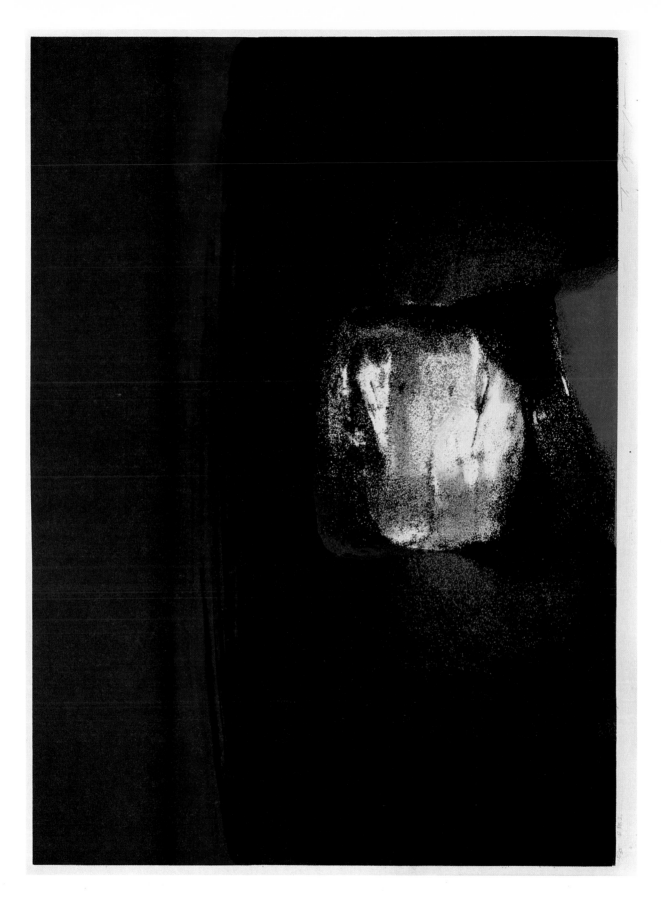

4　AZUMAYA Takemi: *A Solar Eclipse I*. Lithograph. 510 × 700 mm

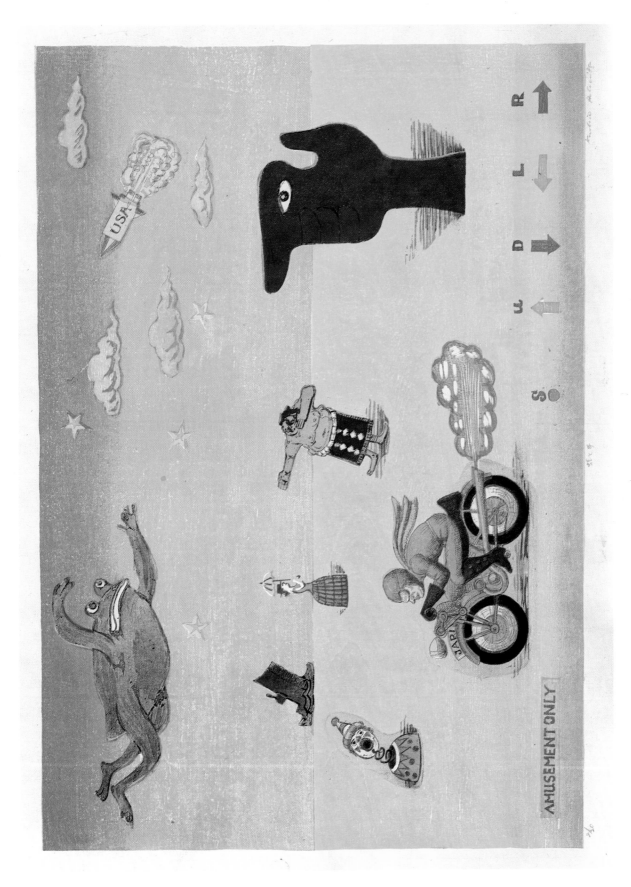

5 BABA Kashiō: *Frog and Hand*. Woodblock/etching/embossing, 460 × 660 mm

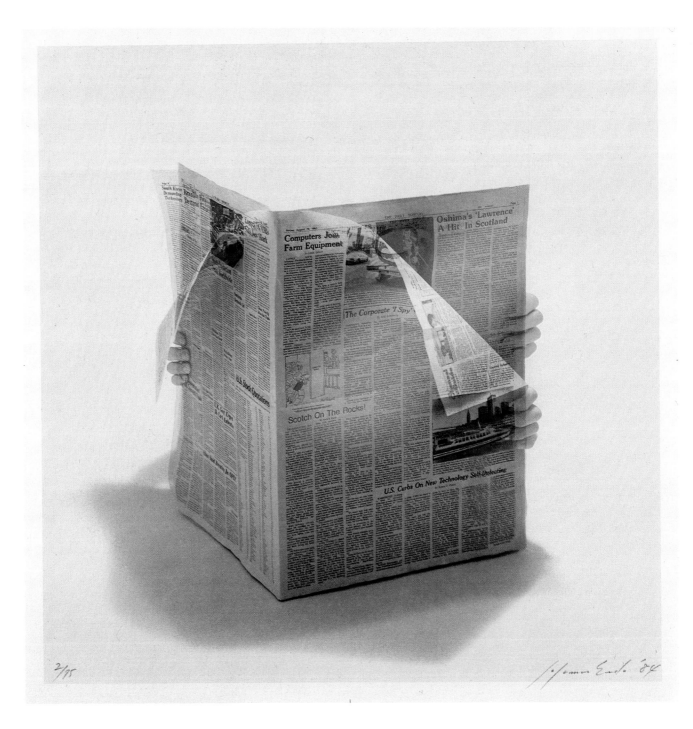

2/75

6 ENDŌ Susumu: *Space and Space – Newspaper*. Offset lithograph, 450 × 450 mm

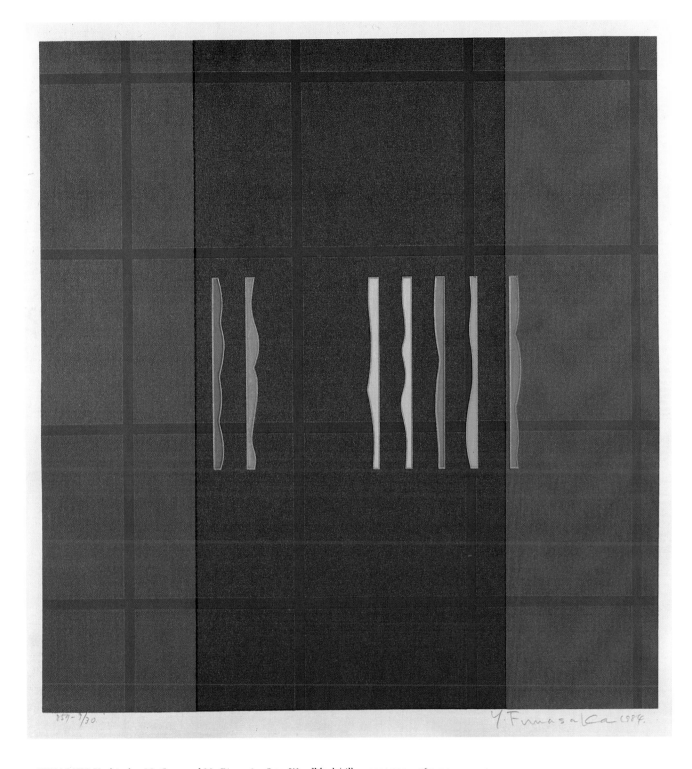

7 FUNASAKA Yoshisuke: *My Space and My Dimension 857*. Woodblock/silkscreen, 590 × 560 mm

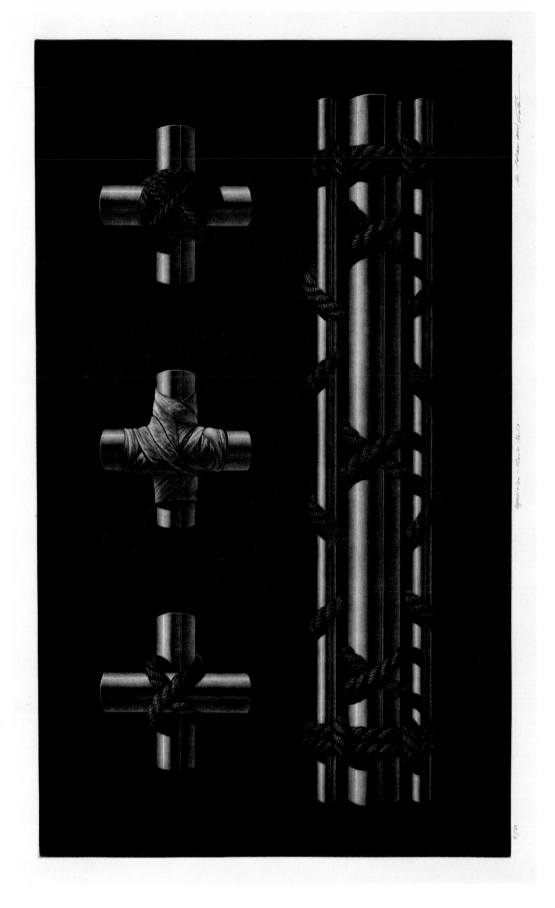

8 HAMANISHI Katsunori: *Opposition – Work No. 13*. Mezzotint. 360 × 600 mm

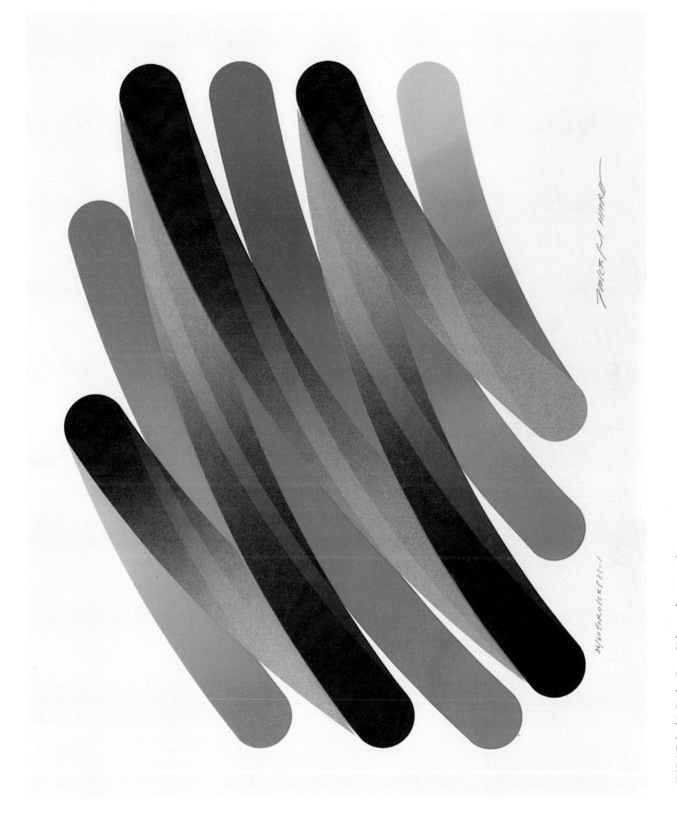

9 HARA Takeshi: *Strokes 85-1*. Lithograph. 570 × 760 mm

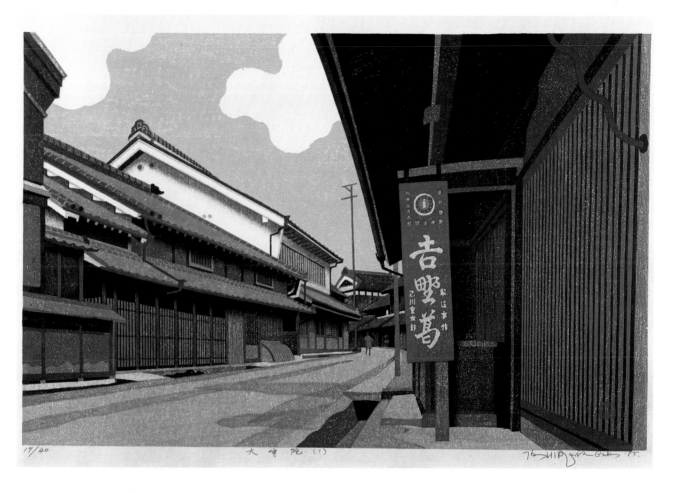

17/40　　　　　　　　　　　　　　大宇陀 (1)

10　HIRONAGA Takehiko: *Ōuda (1)*. Woodblock, 450 × 695 mm

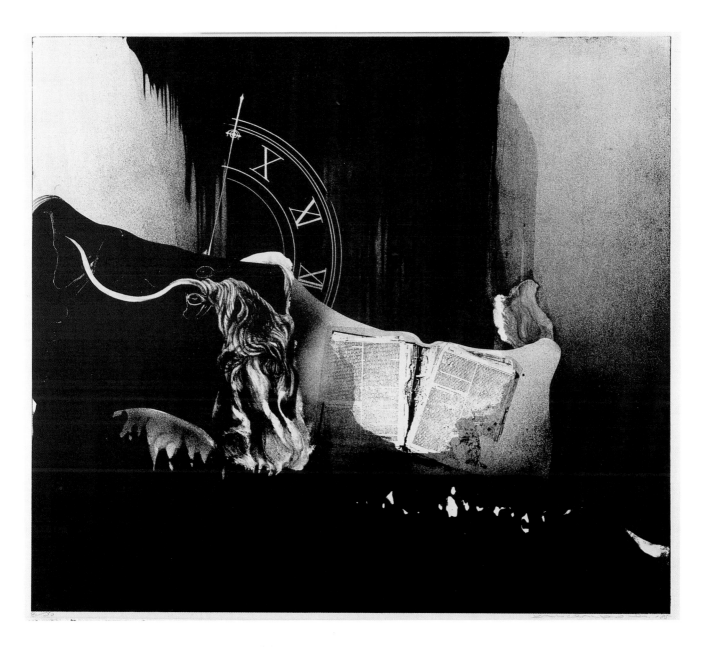

11 HOSHINO Michiko: *Babel the Library; Sand the Book.* Lithograph, 550 × 630 mm

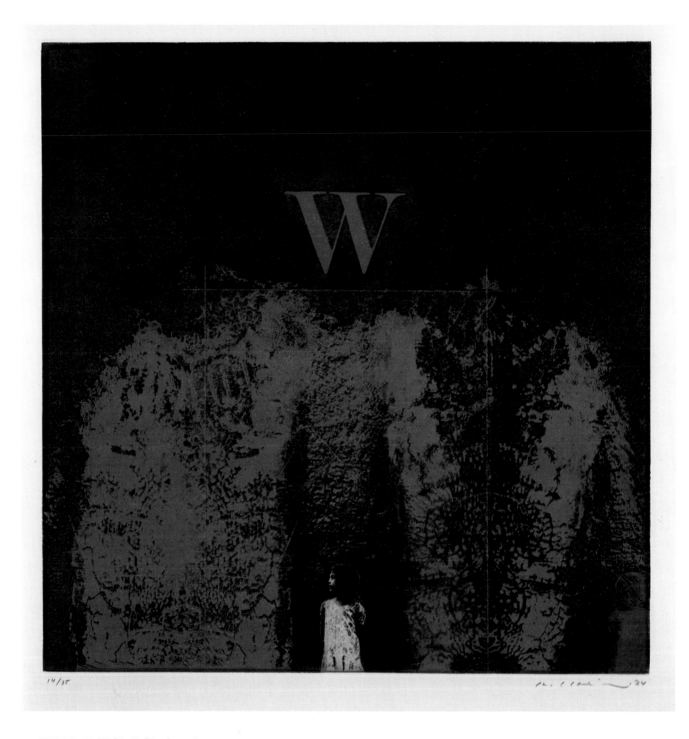

12 IKEDA Ryōji: *Within*. Etching/aquatint, 490 × 490 mm

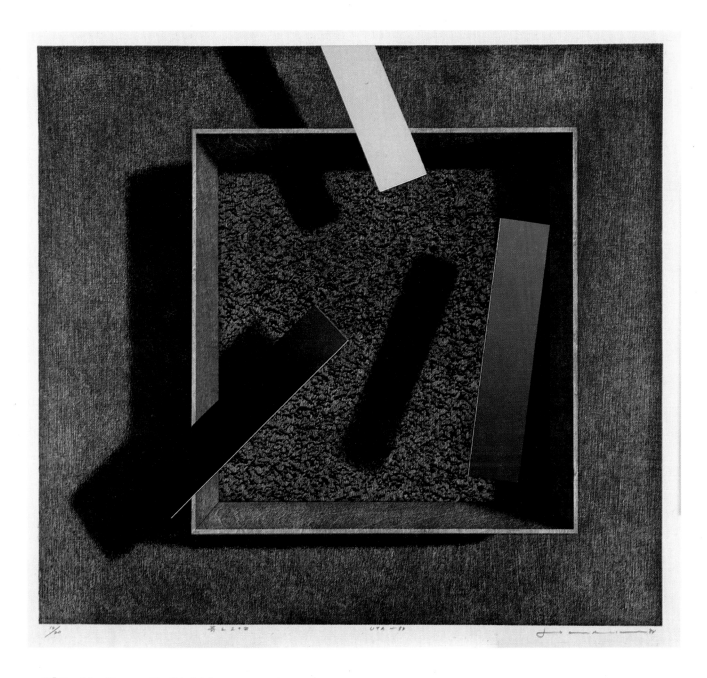

13 ITŌ Handoku: *Uta – 34.* Woodblock/silkscreen, 510 × 570 mm

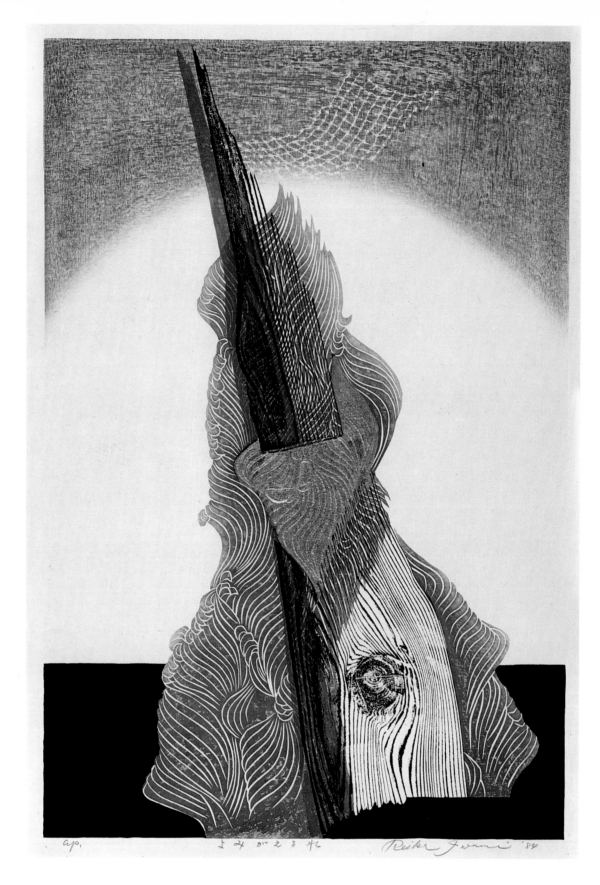

14 IWAMI Reika: *Reviving Water.* Woodblock/embossing, 780 × 525 mm

15 JOHNSON Margaret: *Yesterday's Memory*. Intaglio/embossing, 415×545 mm

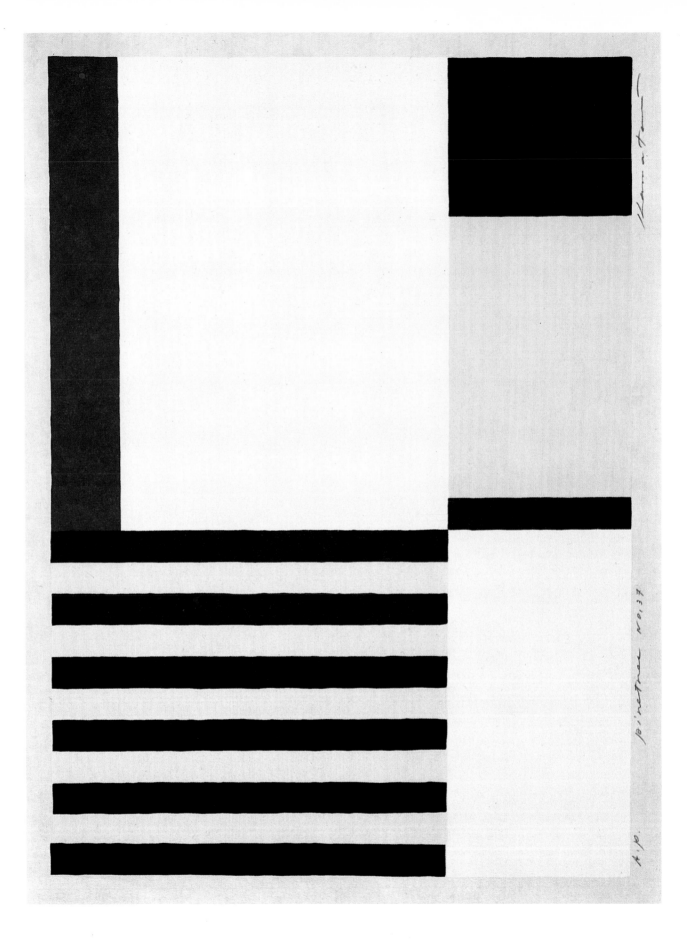

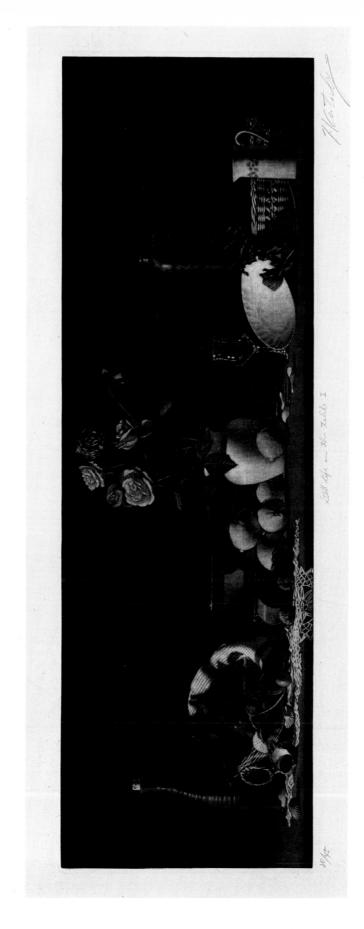

16 KAMATANI Shin'ichi: *Pinetree No. 37.* Silkscreen, 380 × 520 mm

17 KATORI Takeshi: *Still Life on the Table I. Mezzotint,* 215 × 675 mm

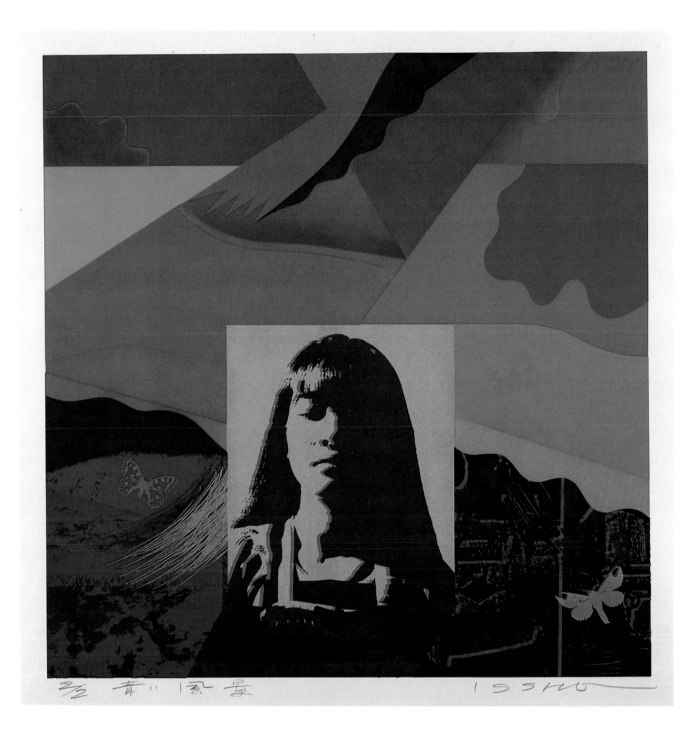

18 KAWABE Isshū: *Blue Scenery.* Silkscreen, 500 × 500 mm

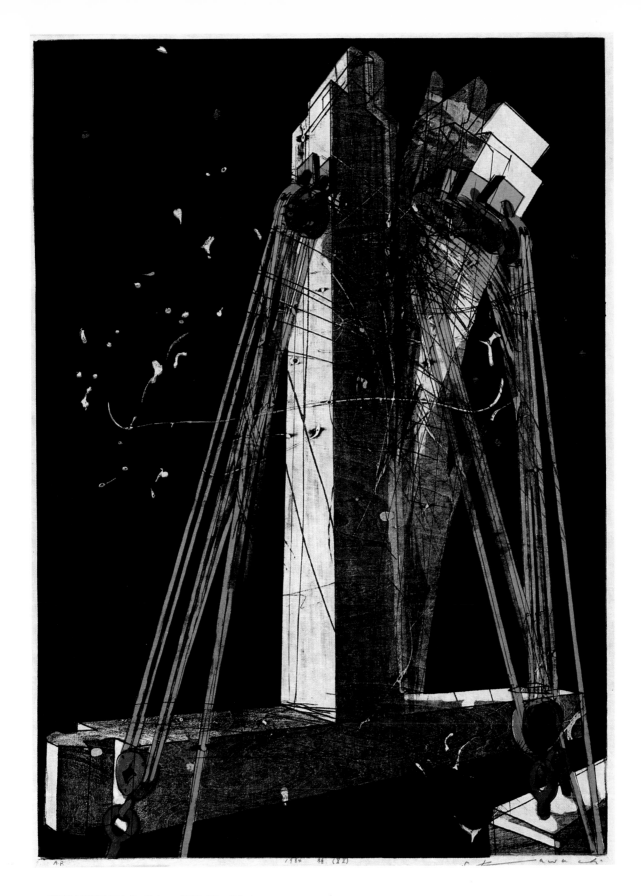

19 KAWACHI Seikō: *'84 Katsura (XII)*. Woodblock, 715 × 510 mm

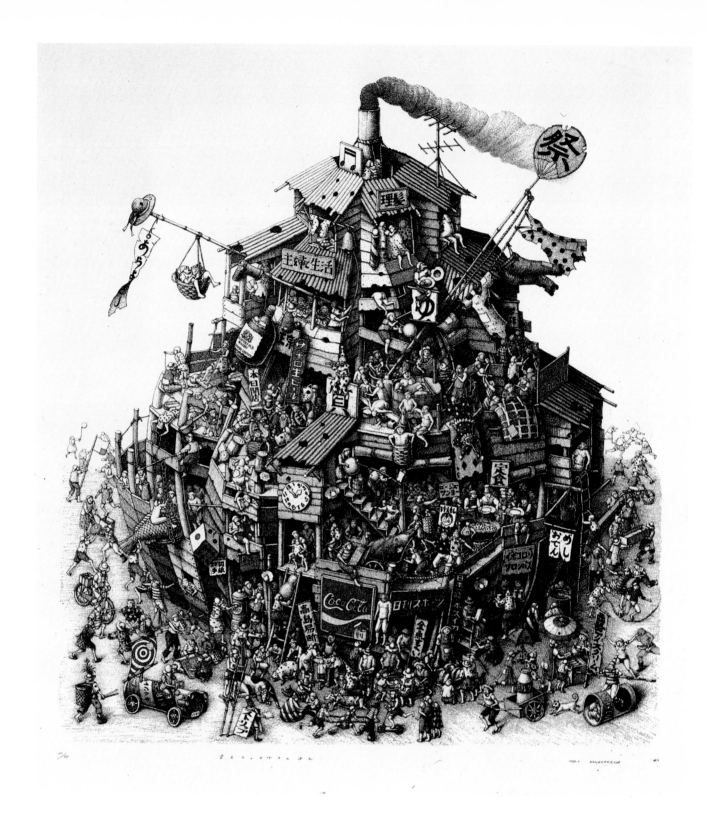

20 KAWAHARADA Tōru: *Pumpkin Paradise of the Poor*. Etching, 400 × 365 mm

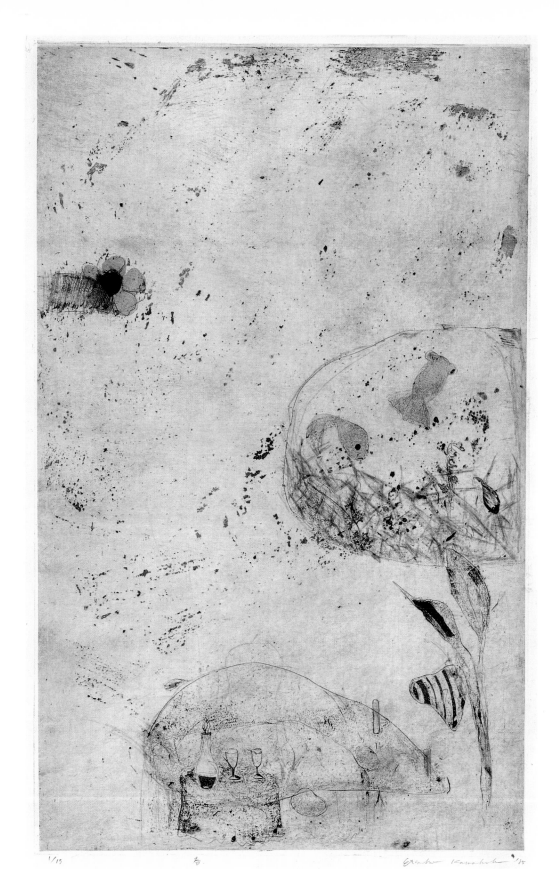

21 KAWAKUBO Etsuko: *Spring.* Lithograph, 730 × 450 mm

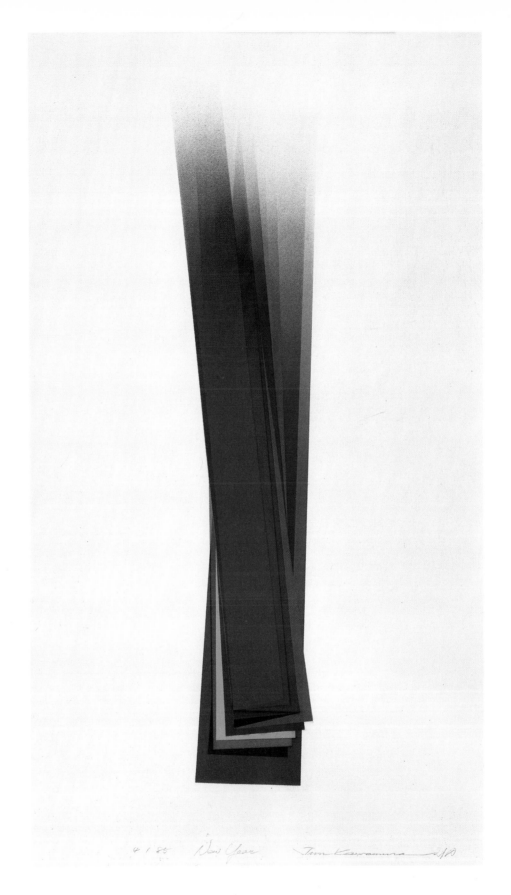

22 KAWAMURA Jun: *New Year*. Silkscreen, 790 × 460 mm

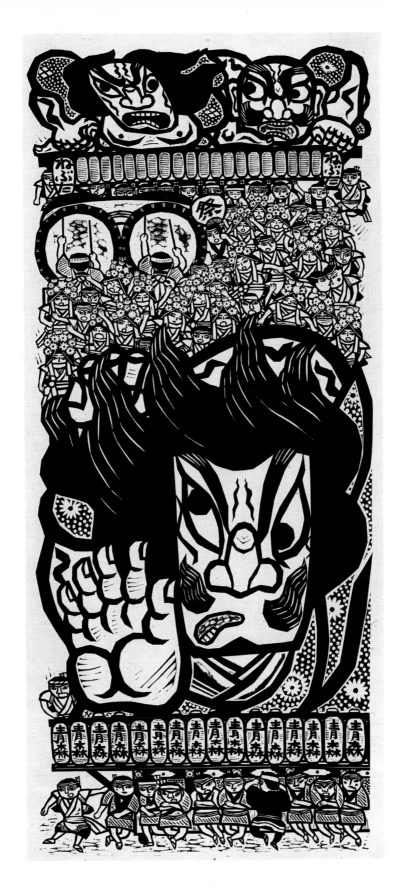

23 KIDA Yasuhiko: *Nebuta Festival I.* Woodblock, 735 × 355 mm

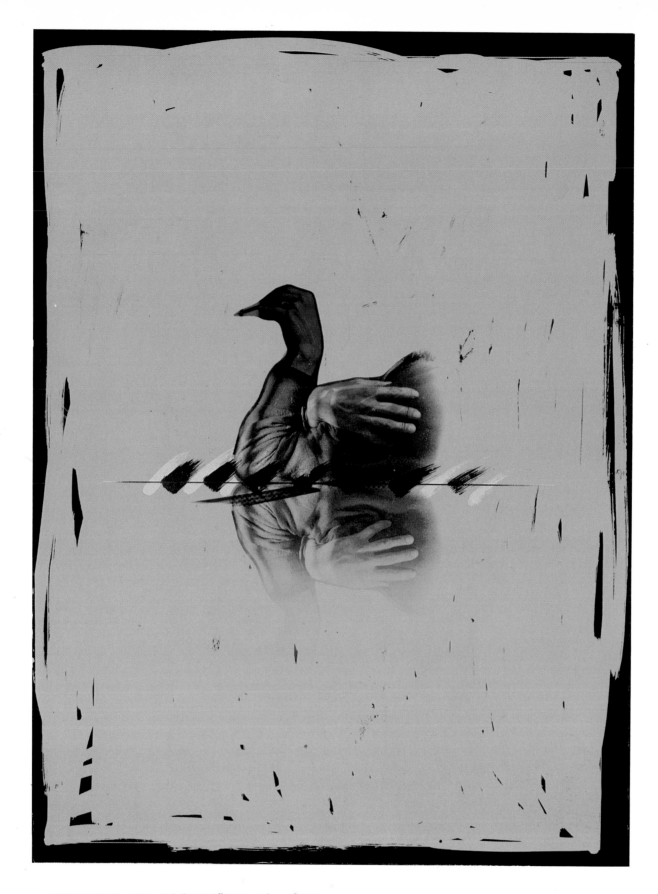

24 KIMURA Hideki: *A Waterbird of Mr I.* Silkscreen, 760 × 560 mm

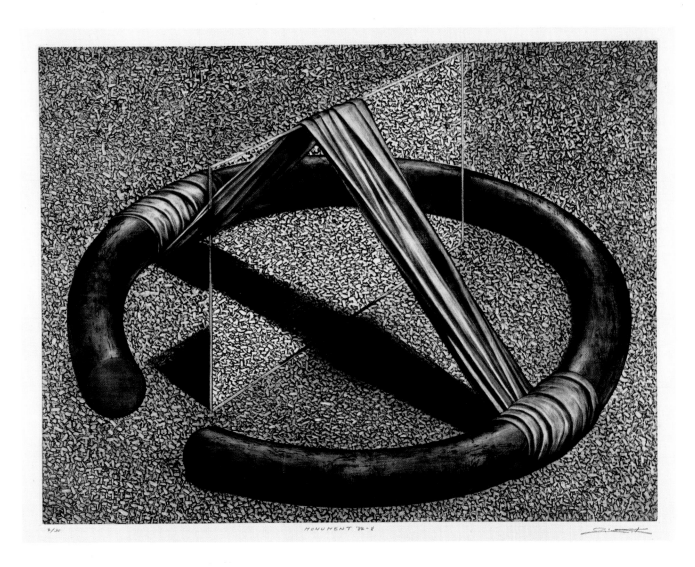

25 KOBAYASHI Jinan: *Monument '84-S.* Etching/mezzotint, 450 × 595 mm

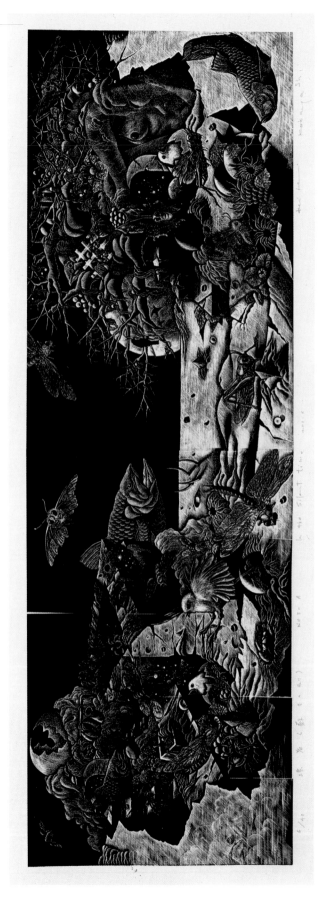

26 KOBAYASHI Keisei: *In the Silent Time No. 3-A.* Wood engraving. 205 × 625 mm

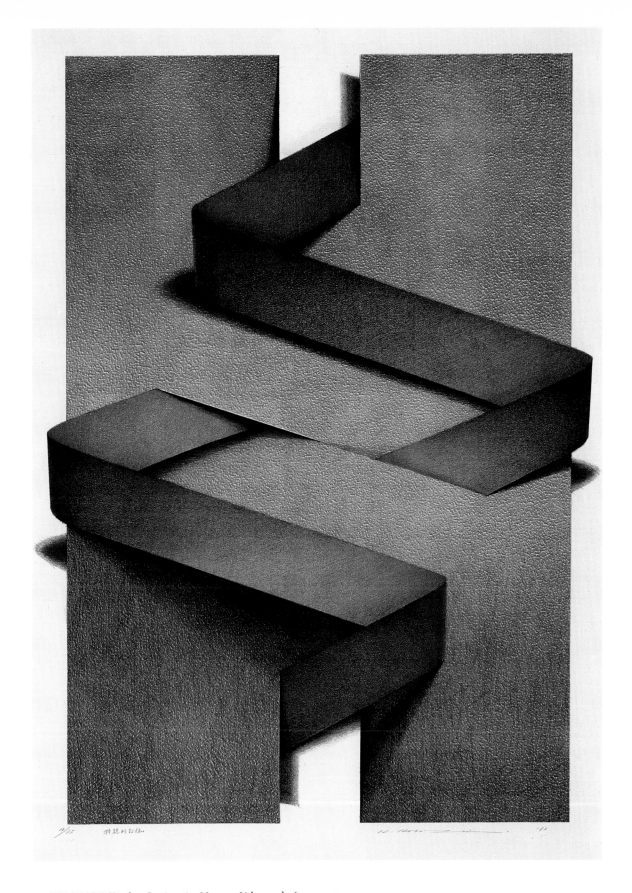

27 KOBAYASHI Kiyoko: *Continuative Memory*. Lithograph, 650 × 490 mm

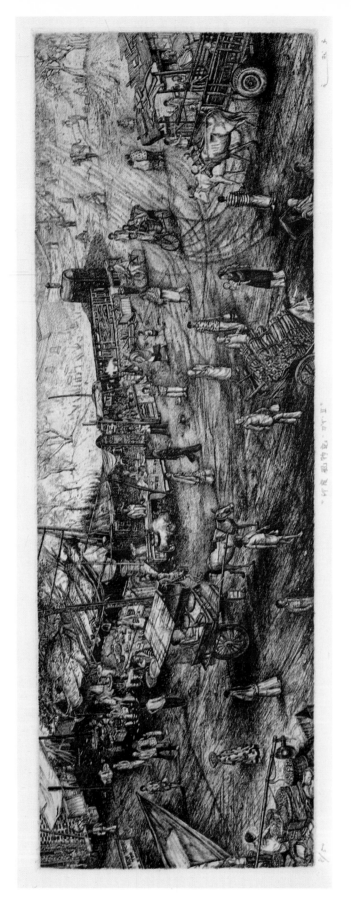

28 KURITA Mariko: *Scenes and Manners in India – Gaya II*. Etching. 150 × 415 mm

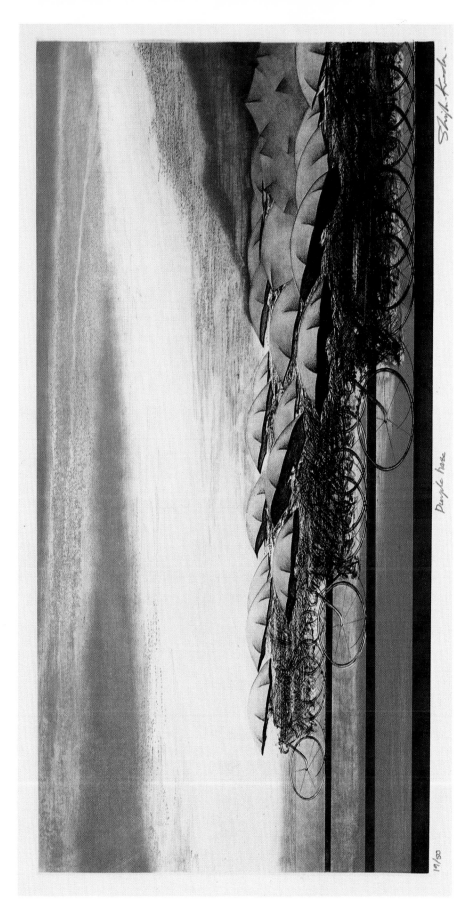

29 KURODA Shigeki: *Purple Haze*. Etching/aquatint. 295 × 595 mm

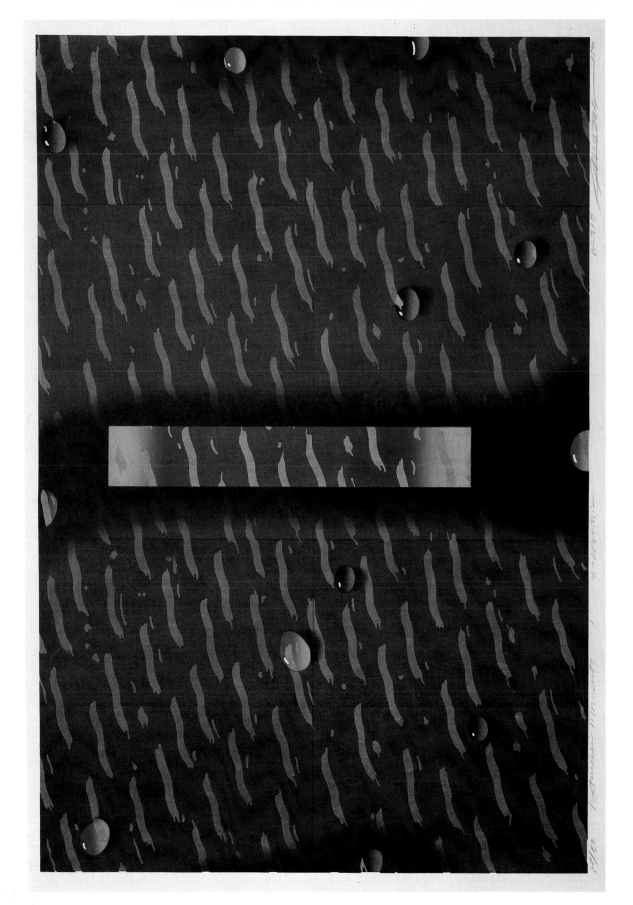

30 KUROSAKI Akira: *Between Moments 1*. Woodblock. 560 × 820 mm

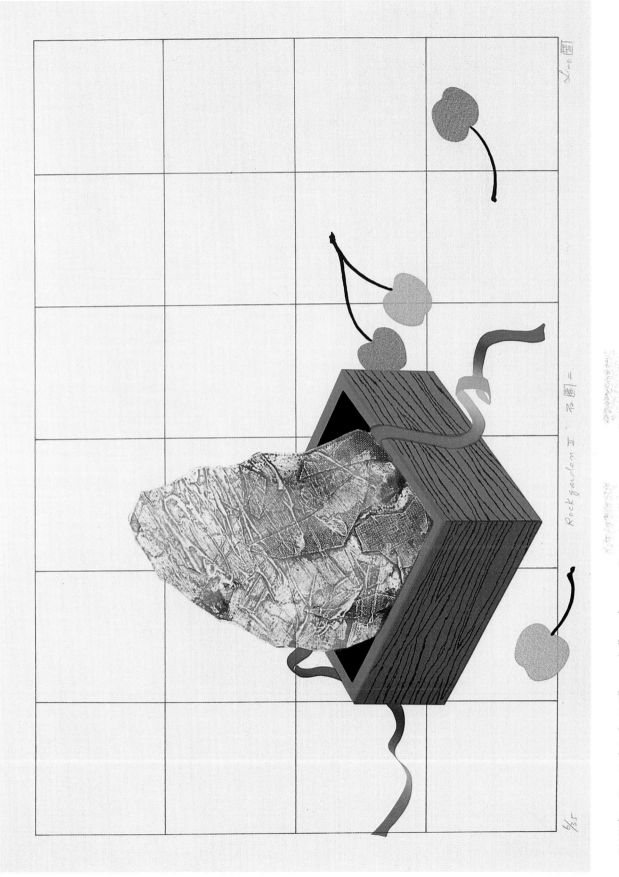

31 LIAO Shiou-Ping: *Rock Garden II.* Silkscreen/collagraph. 330 × 480mm

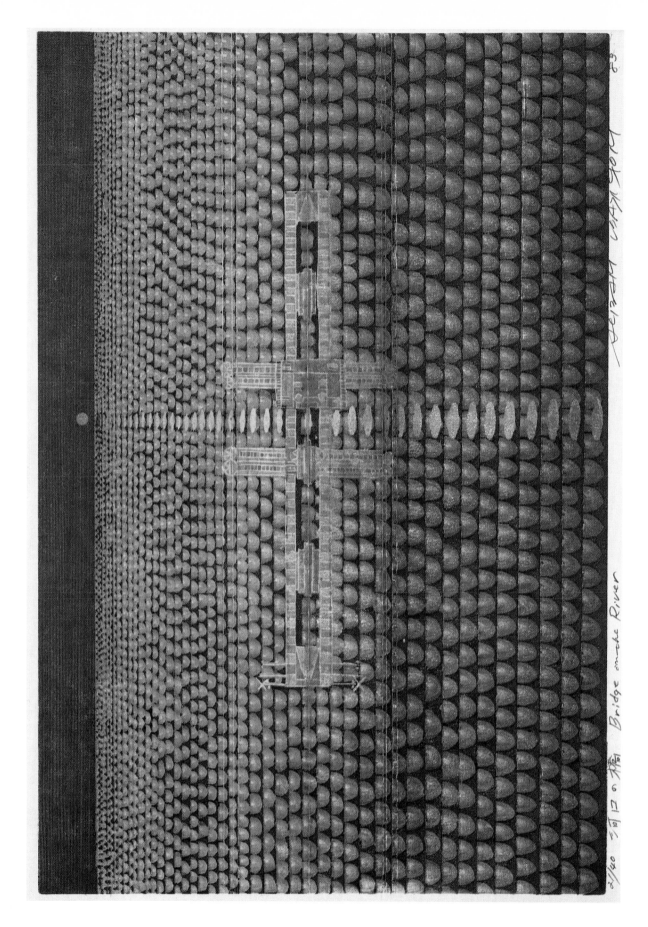

32 MAEDA Morikazu: *Bridge on the River*. Woodblock. 335 × 490 mm

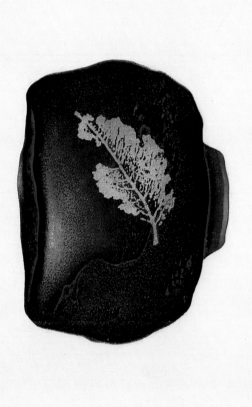

33 MAKI Haku: *Collection 85-10*. Cement/mortar/woodblock. 135 × 350mm

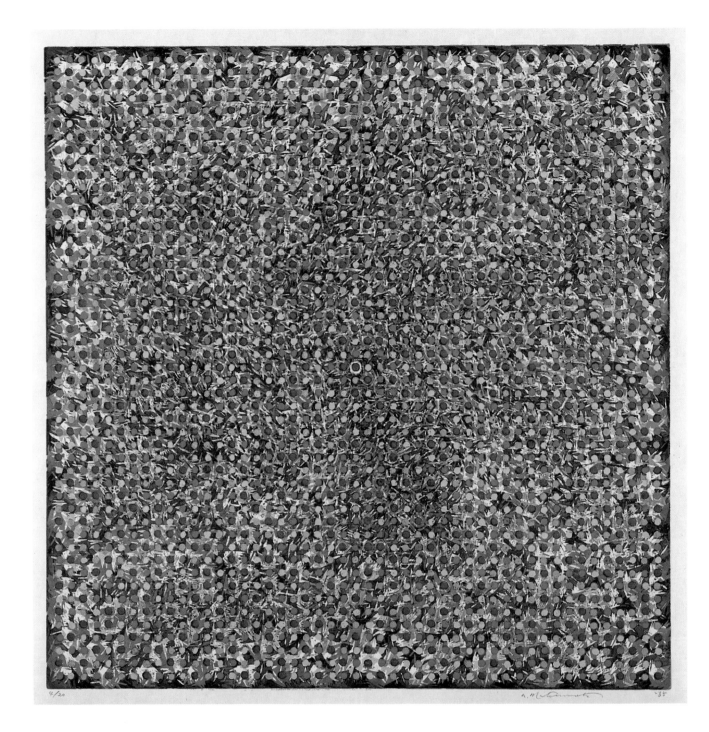

34 MATSUMOTO Akira: *Revolve (W5-Negative/Positive)*. Woodblock, 600 × 600 mm

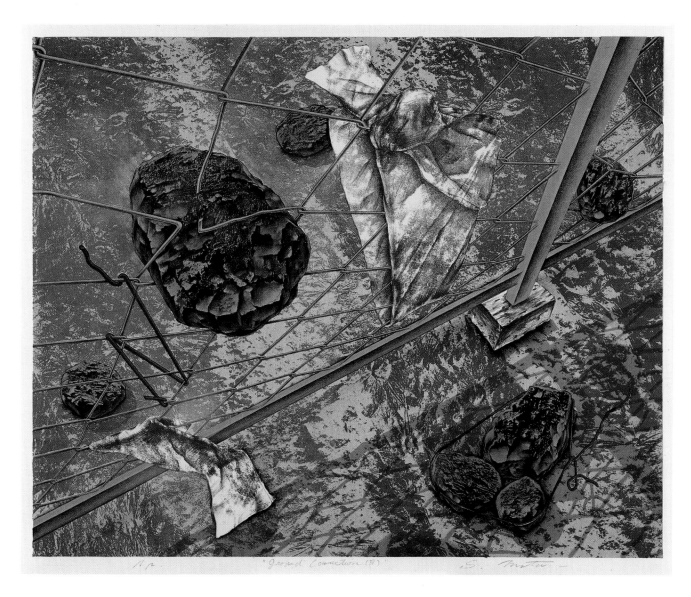

35 MATSUMURA Sei'ichi: *Ground Connection (IV)*. Lithograph, 500 × 630 mm

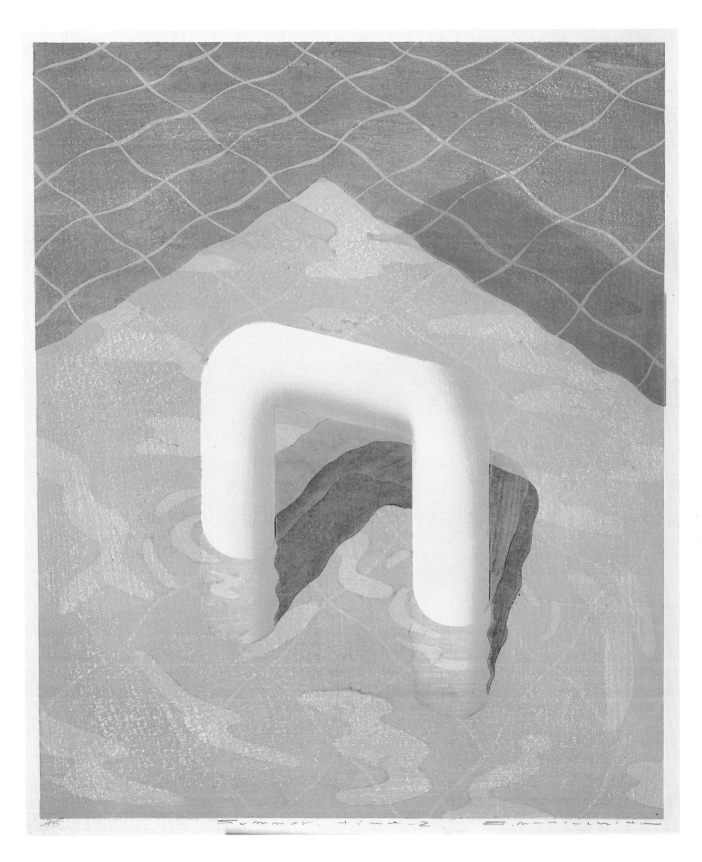

36 MATSUSHITA Satoru: *Summer Time – 2*. Woodblock, 600 × 500 mm

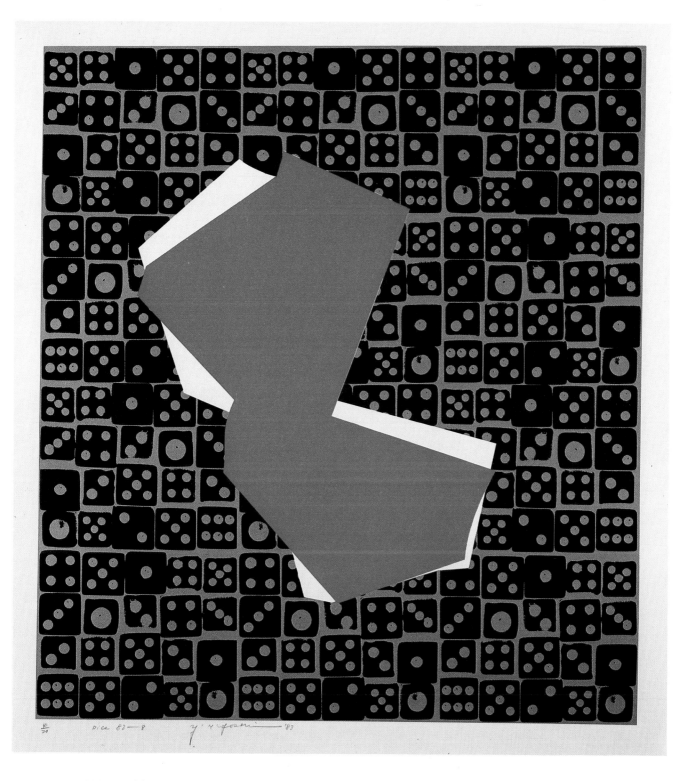

37 MIYOSHI Yukiko: *Dice 83-8*. Silkscreen, 530 × 485 mm

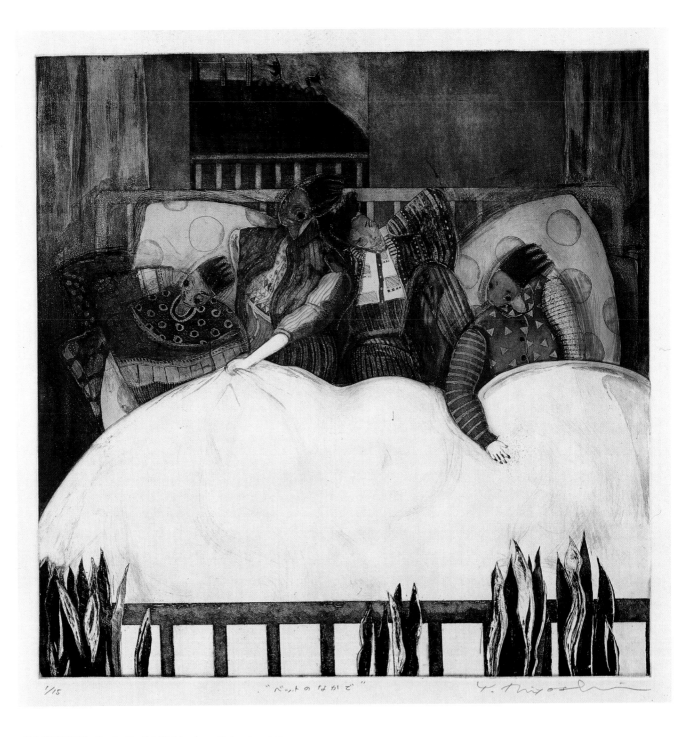

1/15   "ベットのなかで"   Y. Miyoshi

38 MIYOSHI Yuriko: *In the Bed.* Etching/aquatint, 450 × 450 mm

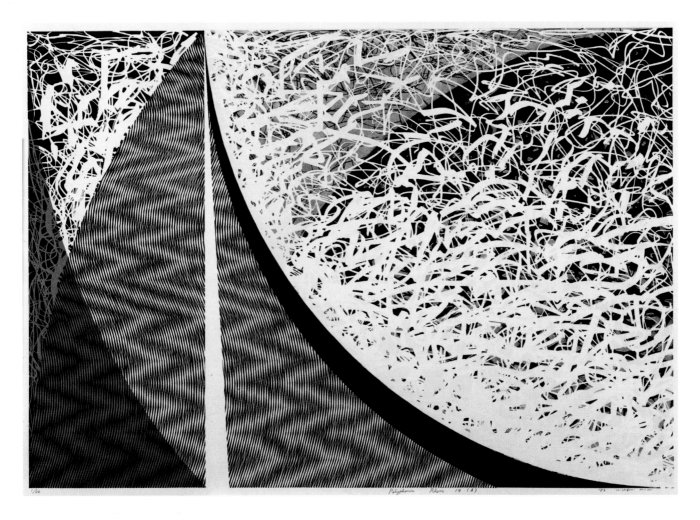

39 MORI Hidefumi: *Polyphonic Plane 14 (A)*. Woodblock, 600 × 795 mm

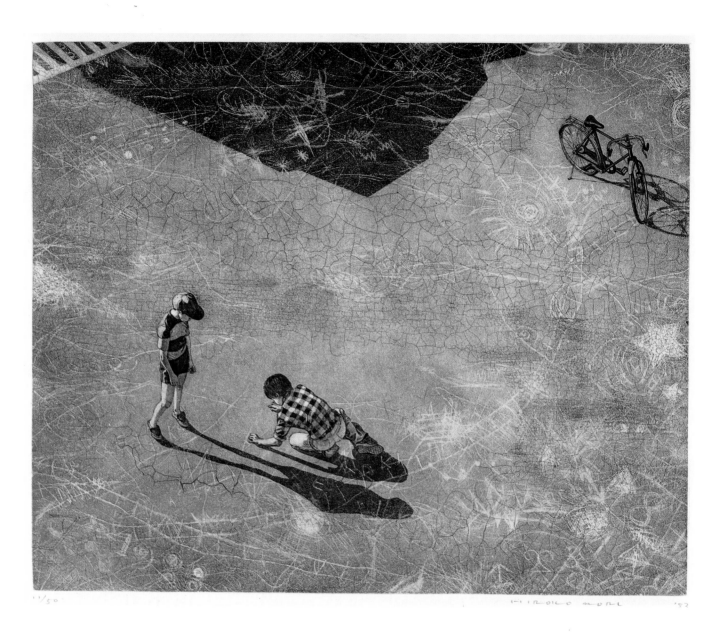

40 MORI Hiroko: *Graffiti.* Etching/aquatint, 360 × 445 mm

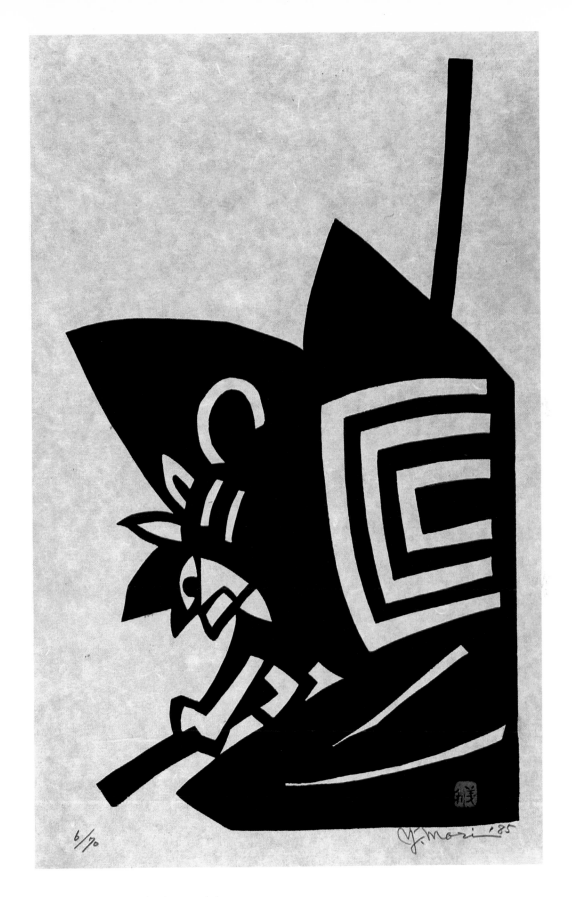

6/70

41 MORI Yoshitoshi: *Shibaraku*. Stencil, 630 × 410 mm

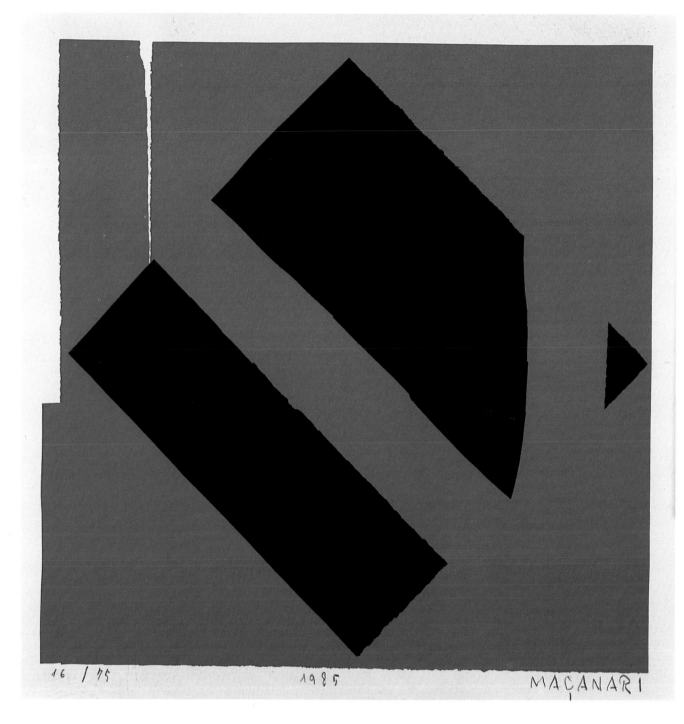

42 MURAI Masanari: *Square*. Silkscreen, 480 × 480 mm

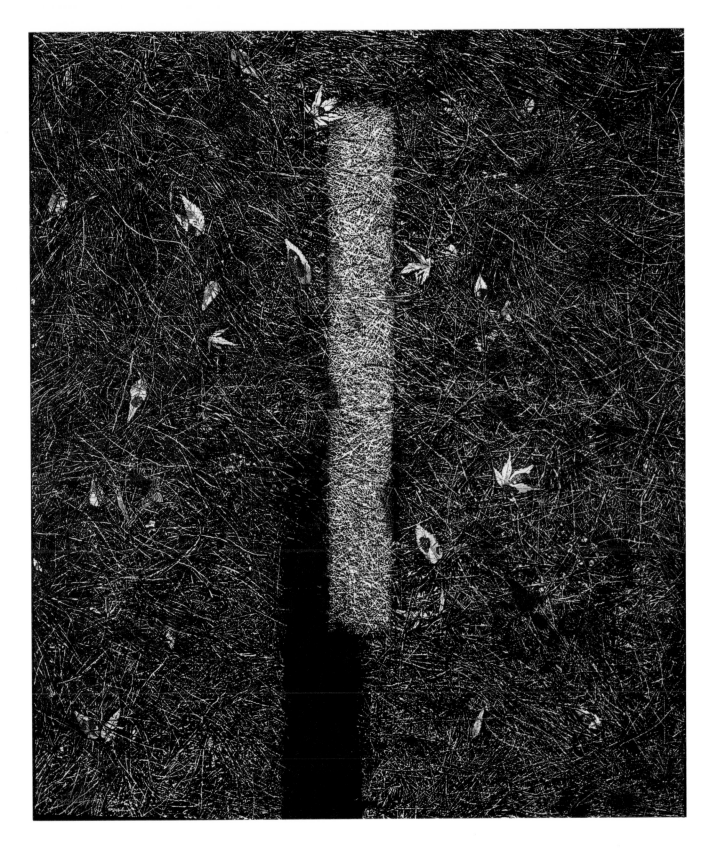

43 NAKABAYASHI Tadayoshi: *Transposition '83 – Ground – I*. Etching/aquatint, 565 × 485 mm

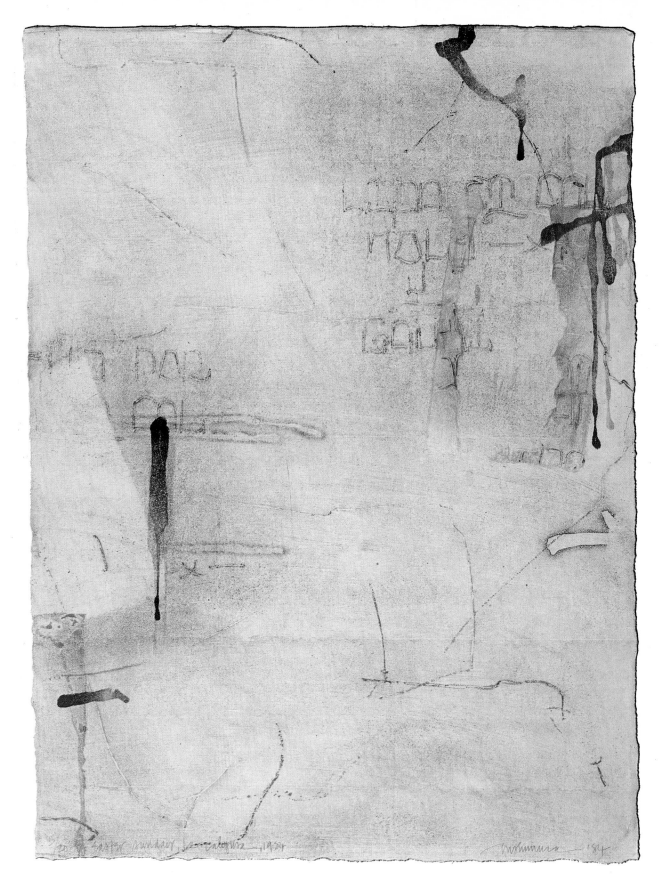

44 NISHIMURA Norine: *Easter Sunday, La Califusa, 1984.* Woodblock/*chine collé,* 775 × 550 mm

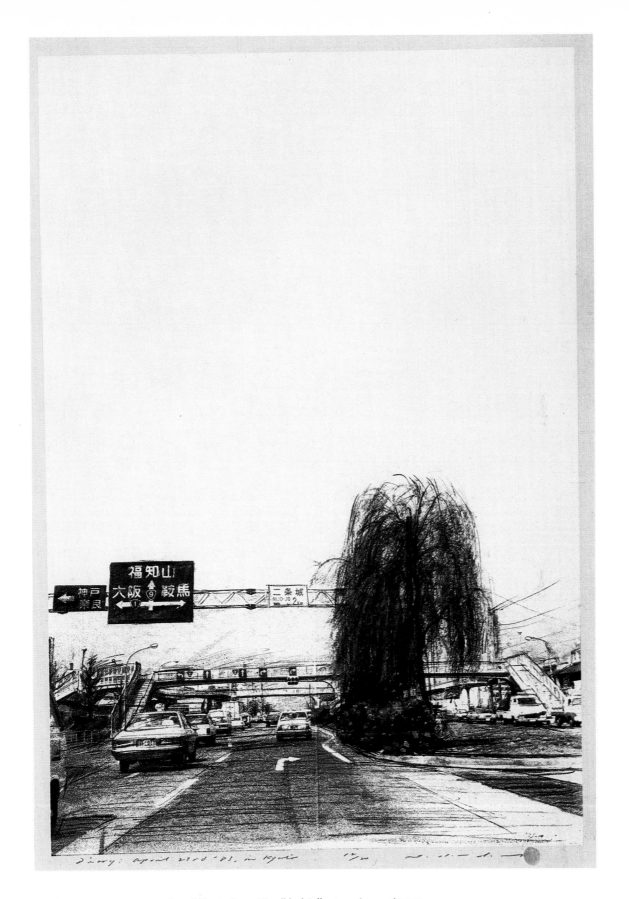

45 NODA Tetsuya: *Diary: April 23rd '83, in Kyoto.* Woodblock/silkscreen. 670 × 460 mm

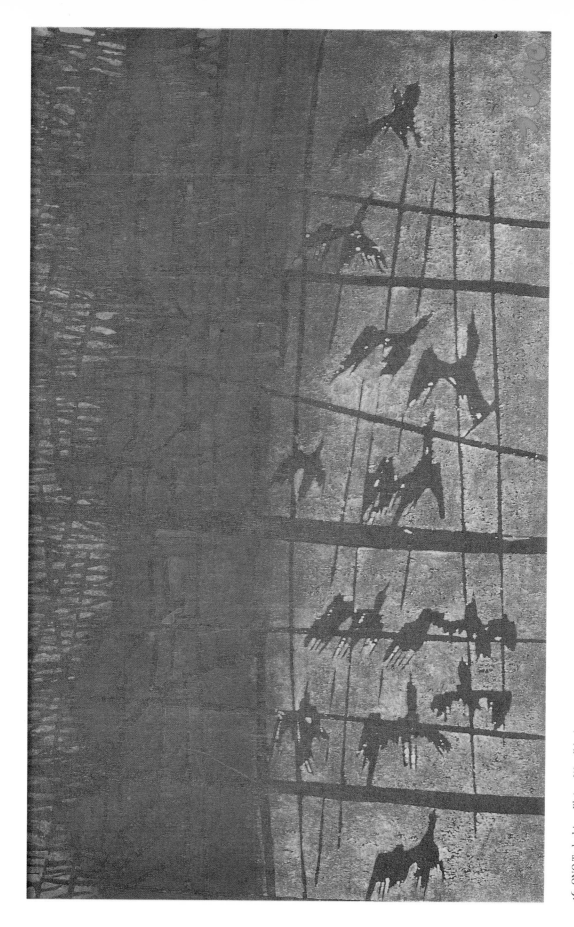

46 ONO Tadashige: *Flying.* Woodblock. 140 × 217 mm

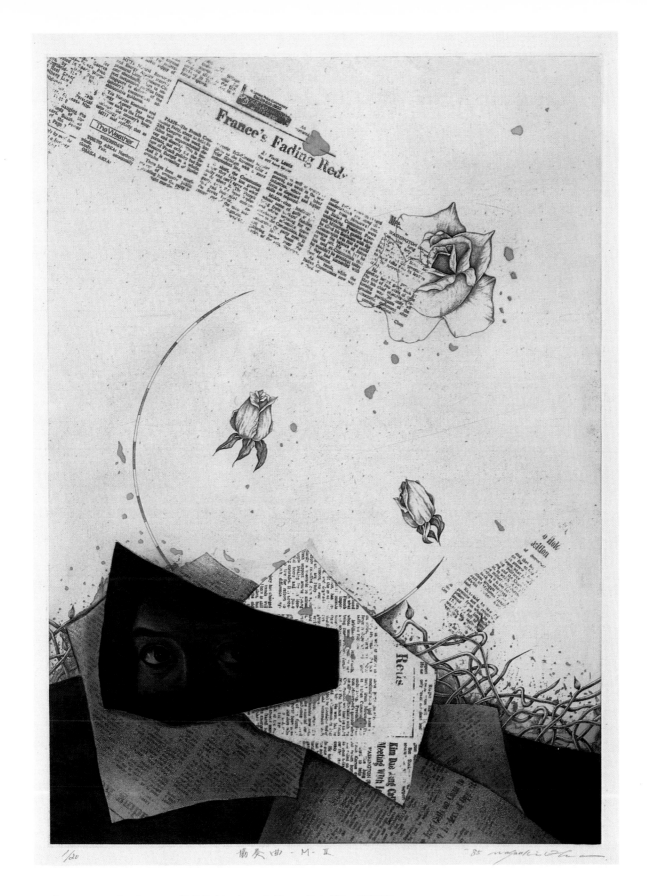

47 ŌNUMA Masaaki: *Concerto – M-II*. Etching/aquatint/mezzotint, 580 × 420 mm

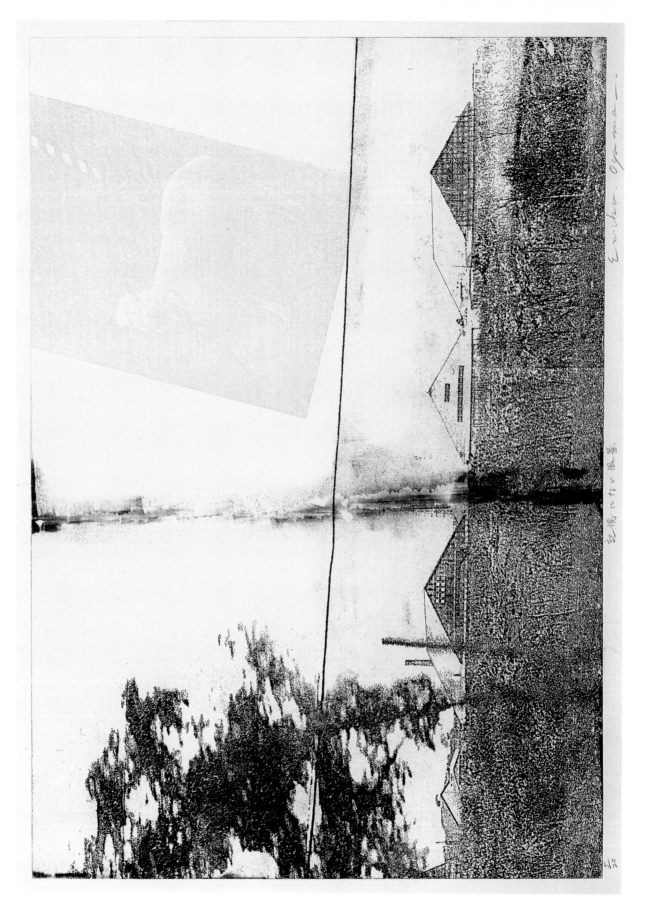

48 ŌYAMA Emiko: *Scenery Unremembered*. Etching. 550 × 785 mm

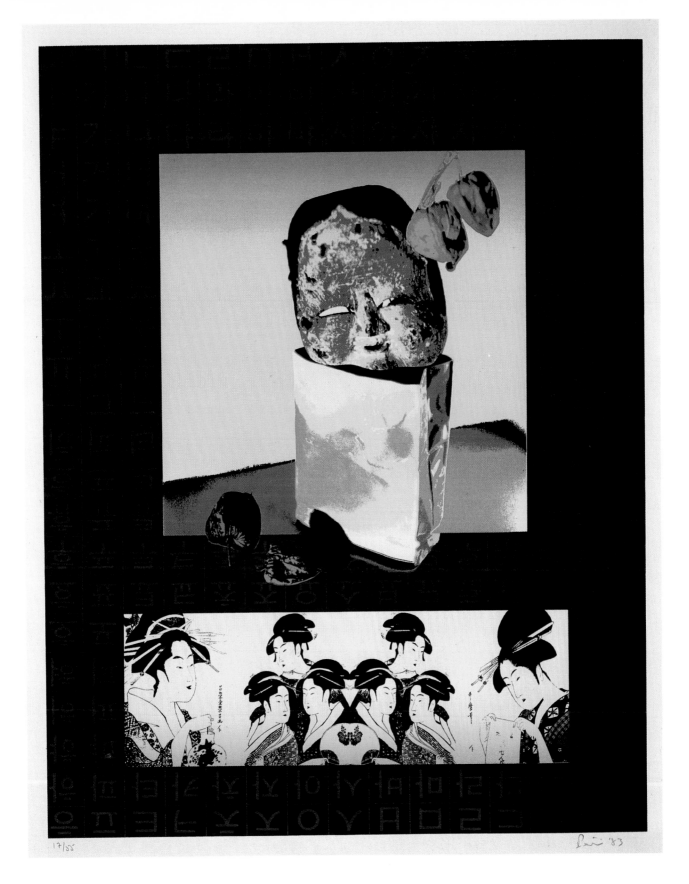

17/55

Petit '83

49 PETIT Gaston: *Invitatoire*. Silkscreen, 590 × 450 mm

3/20   Water in Water No. 9

50 SAHASHI Midori: *Water in Water No. 9*. Etching, 365 × 365 mm

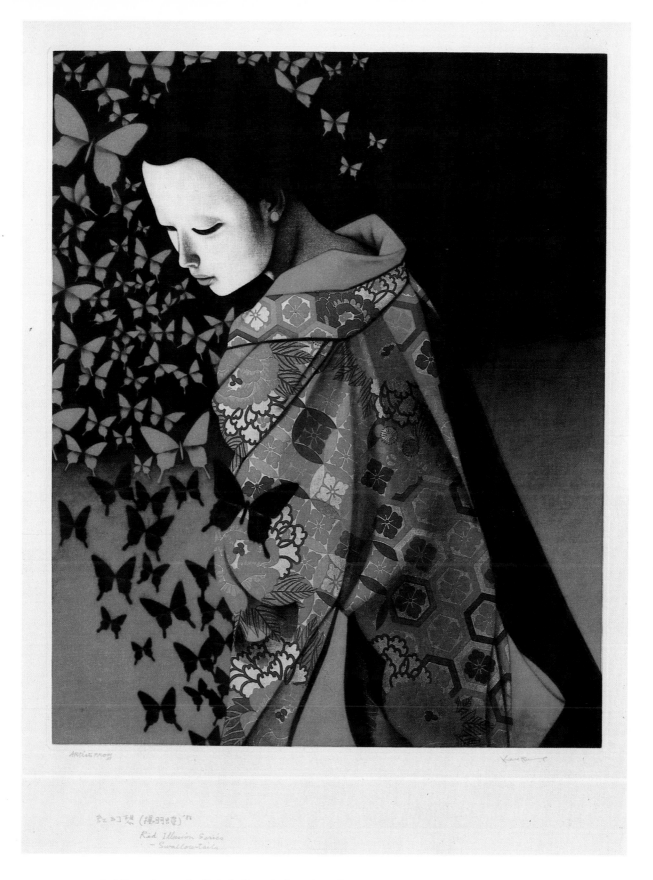

51 SAITO Kaoru: *Red Illusion Series – Swallowtails.* Mezzotint/aquatint, 365 × 300 mm

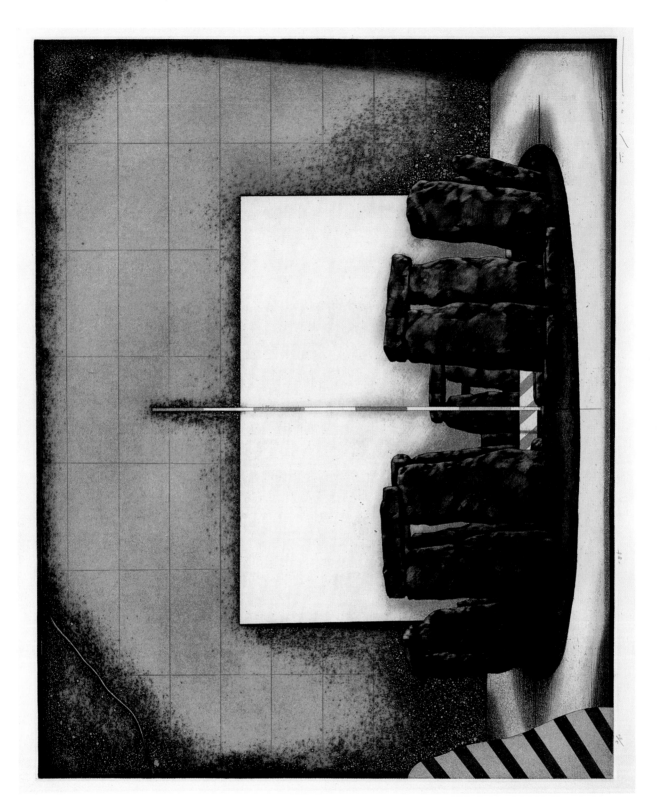

52 SAITŌ Takeshi: *Memory – 85-III.* Etching/aquatint. 450 × 560 mm

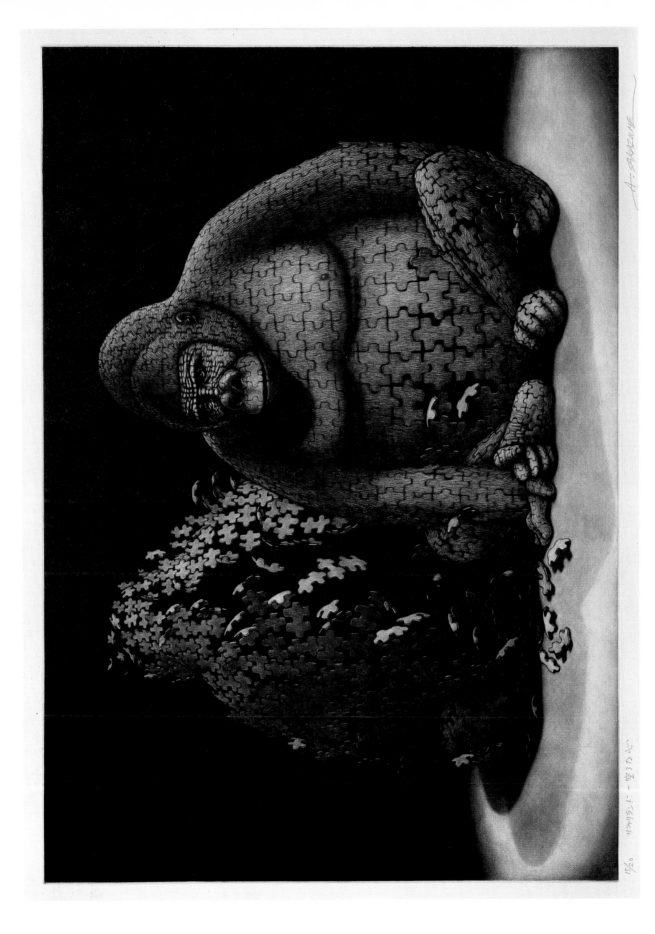

53 SAKAZUME Atsuo: *Safari Land – Empty Heart.* Mezzotint. 590 × 690 mm

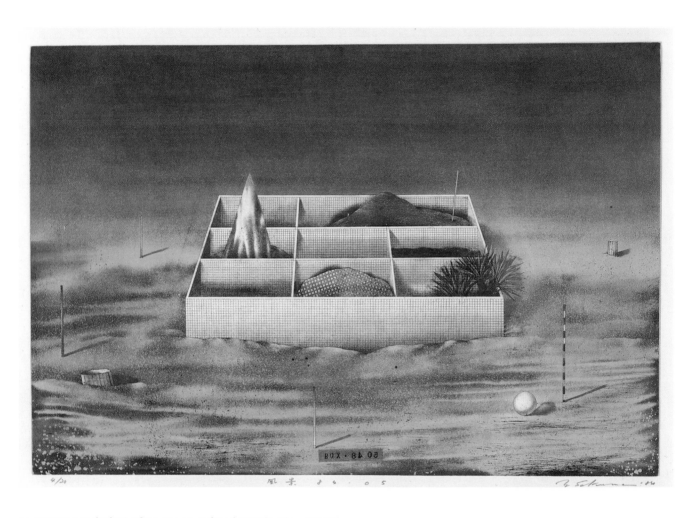

54 SAKUMA Yoshiaki: *Landscape 84-05*. Etching/aquatint, 360 × 550 mm

55 SAWADA Tetsurō: *Brilliant Scape (Blue)*. Silkscreen, 580 × 400 mm

56 SHIMIZU Momo: *Lines No. 104*. Silkscreen. 600 × 800 mm

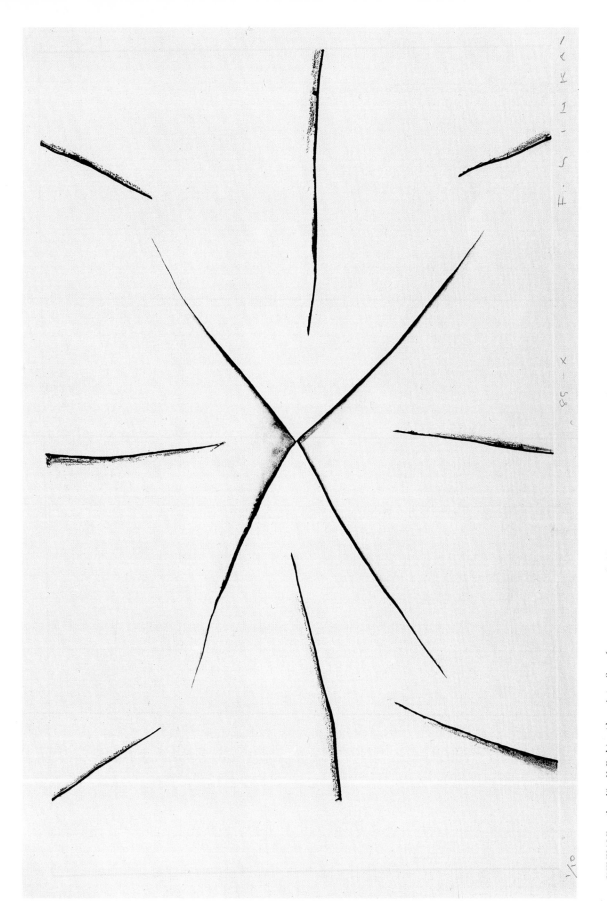

57 SHINKAI Fumiko: '85-X. Etching/drypoint, 485 × 695 mm

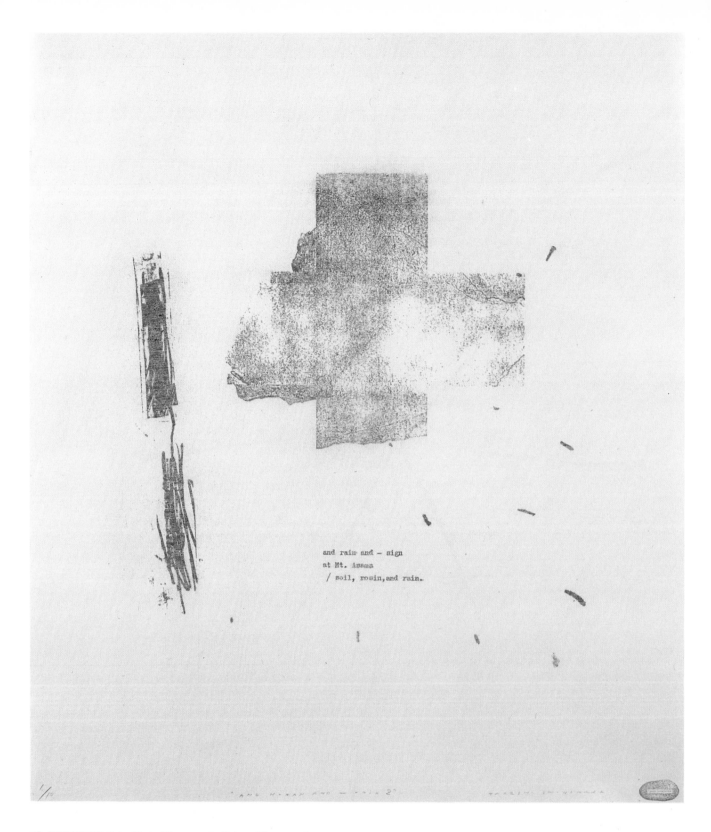

and rain and – sign
at Mt. Asama
/ soil, rosin, and rain.

58 SHINOHARA Takeshi: *And Human and – Rain 2*. Silkscreen, 800 × 700 mm

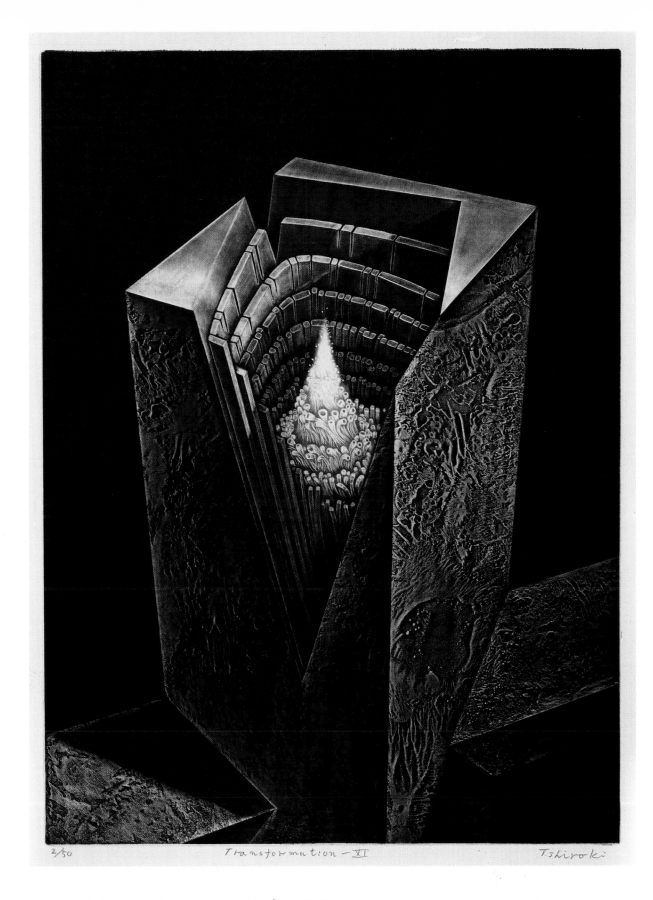

2/50   *Transformation – XI*   Tshiroki

59 SHIROKI Toshiyuki: *Transformation – XI.* Mezzotint, 600 × 450 mm

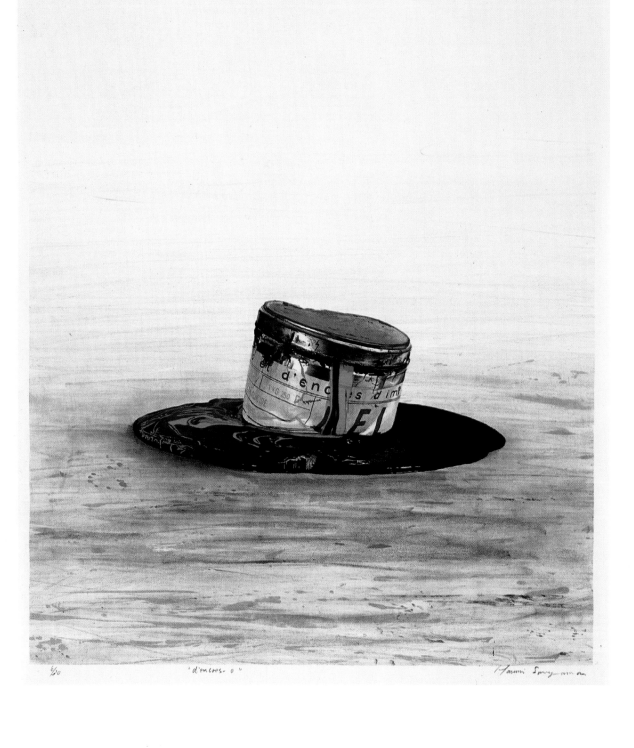

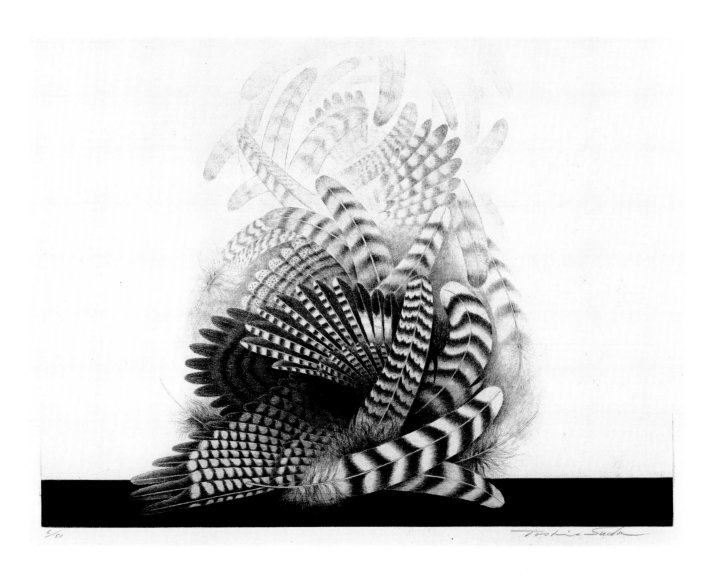

61 SUDA Toshio: *Midnight Sun I.* Etching, 450 × 600 mm

60 SONOYAMA Harumi: *D'encres – O.* Lithograph, 780 × 540 mm

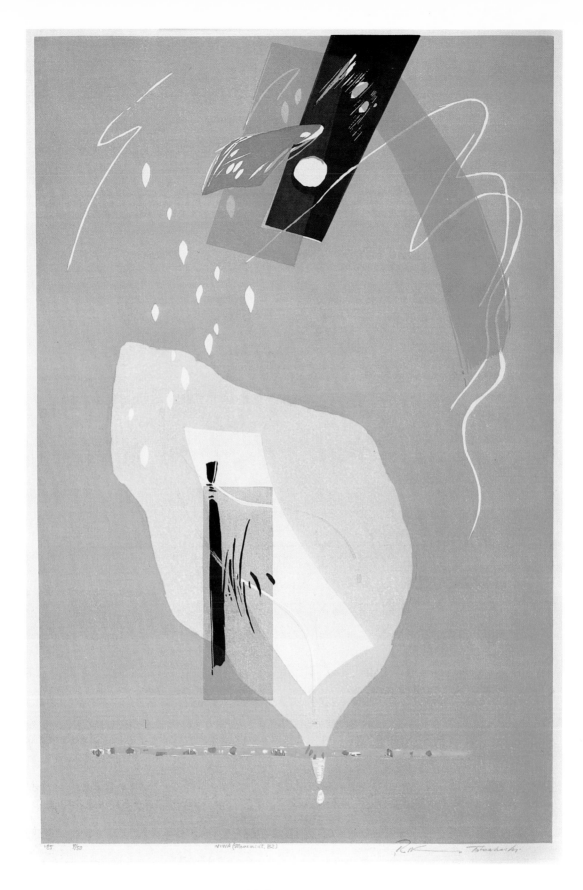

62 TAKAHASHI Rikio: *Niwa (Movement B2)*. Woodblock, 820 × 545 mm

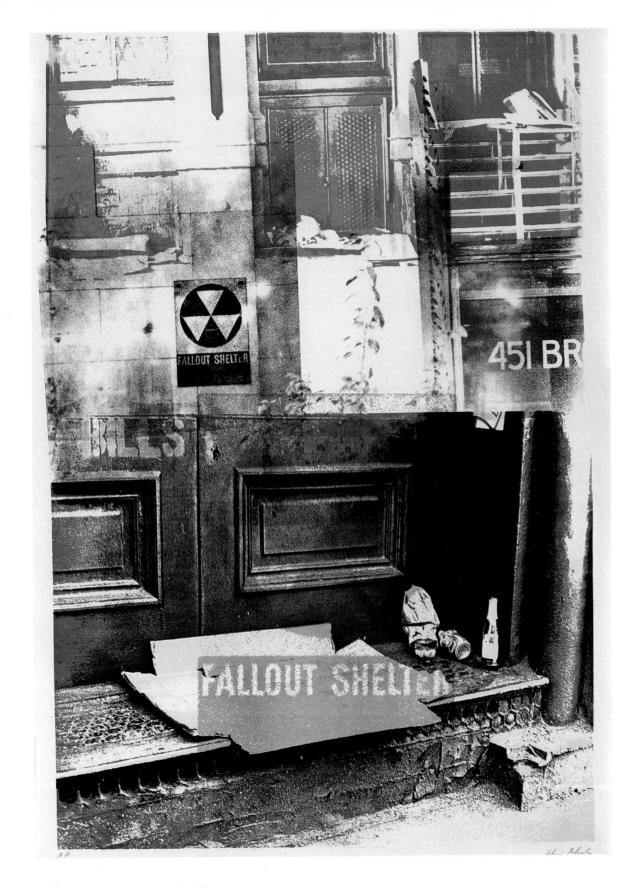

63 TAKEDA Akemi: *Fallout Shelter*. Silkscreen, 740 × 505 mm

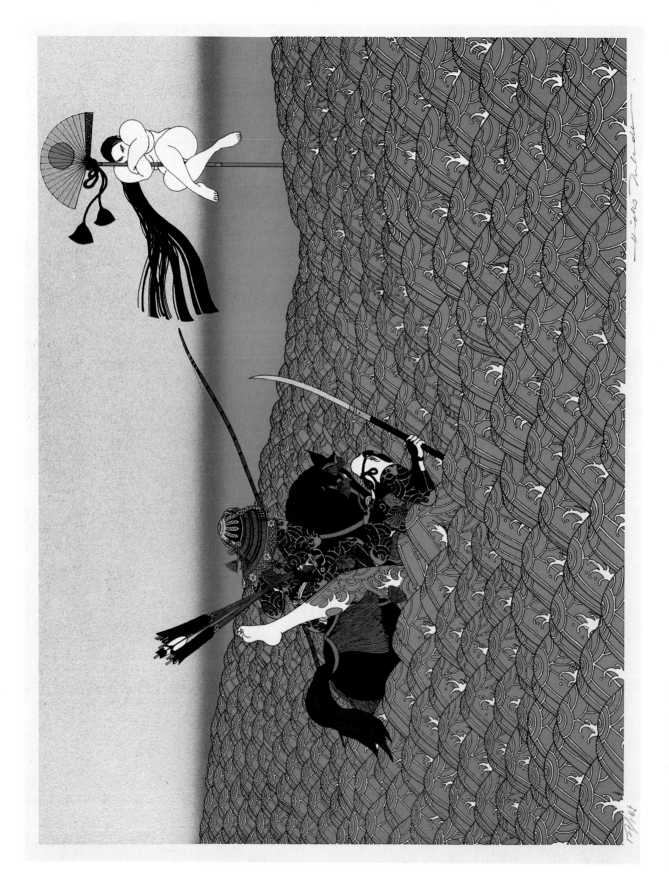

64 TAKEDA Hideo: *Mark of the Fan*. Silkscreen. 395 × 530 mm

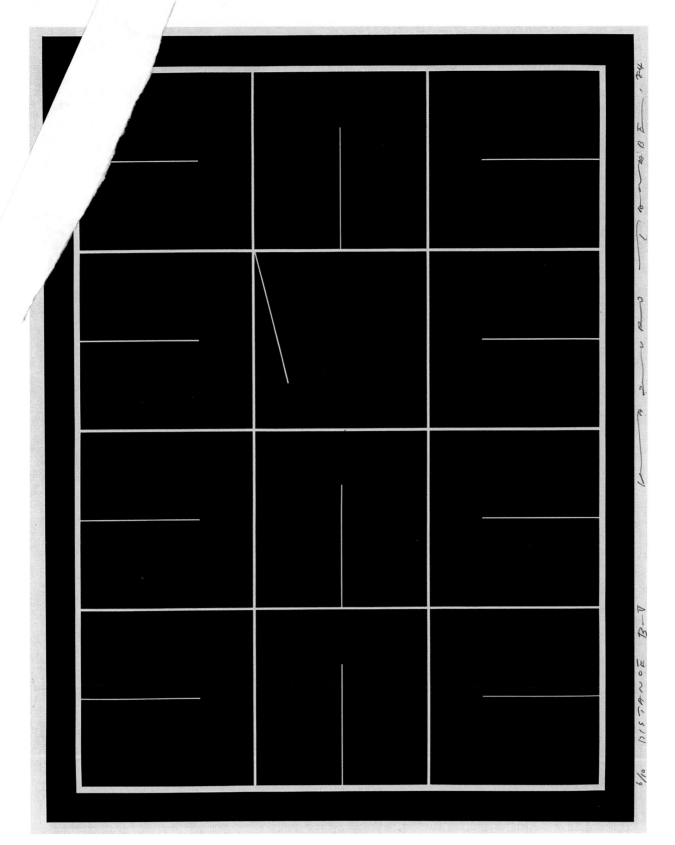

65 TANABE Kazurō: *Distance B-V*. Silkscreen, 400 × 520 mm

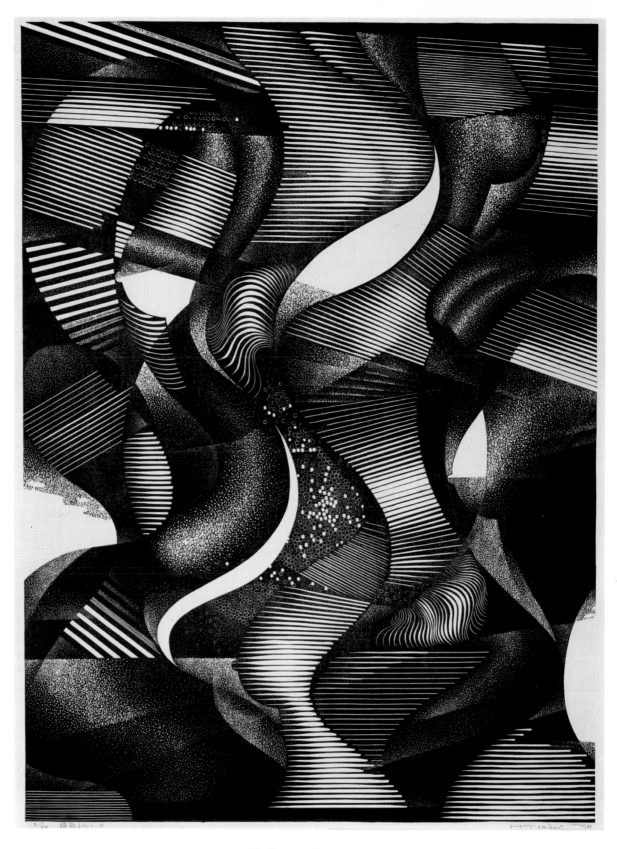

66 TOMIHARI Hiroshi: *In Praise of Torsos – O.* Woodblock, 570 × 765 mm

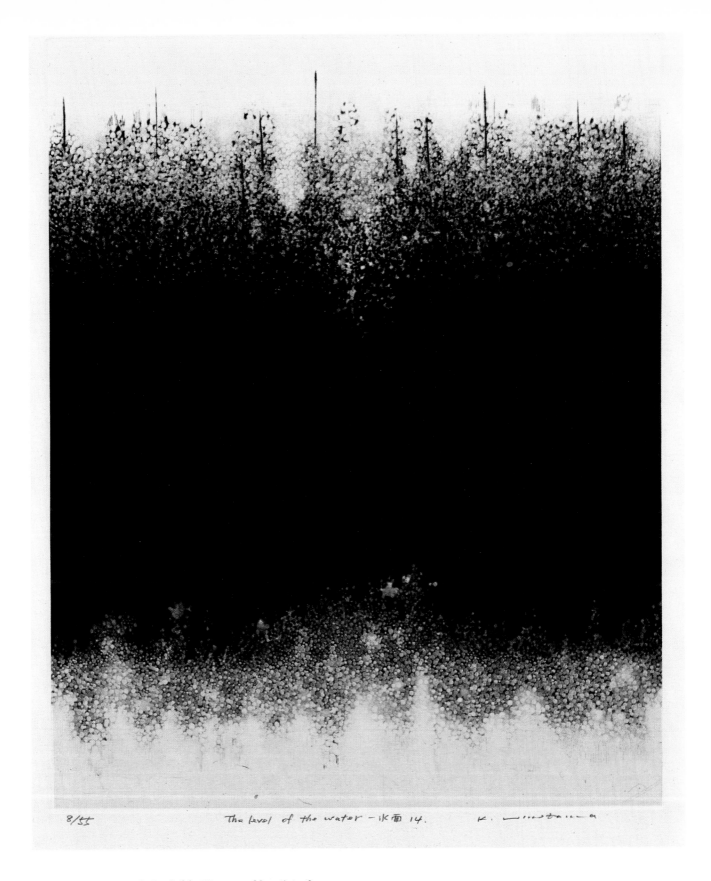

8/55   The level of the water — 水面 14.   K. Umezawa

67 UMEZAWA Kazuo: *The Level of the Water – 14*. Mezzotint, 360 × 300 mm

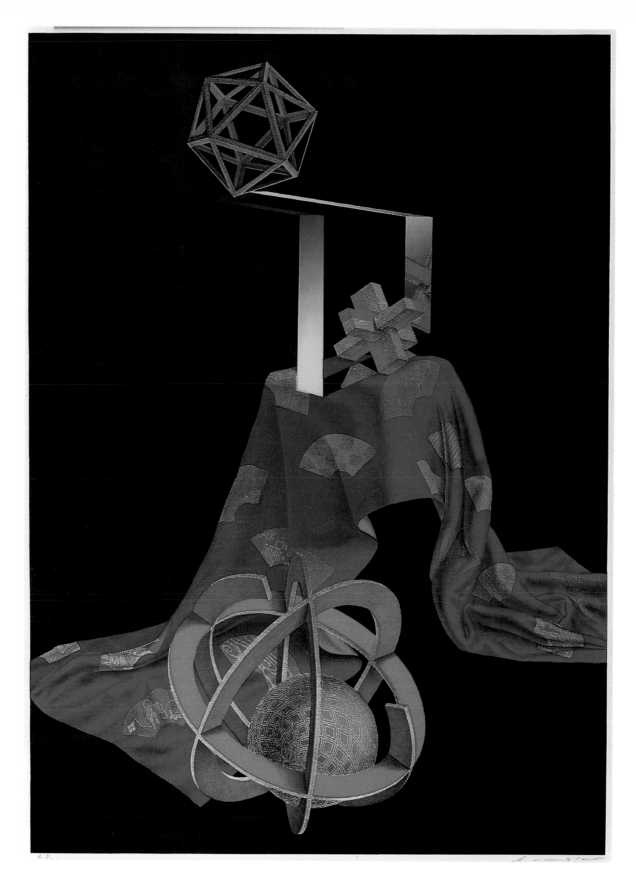

68 WAKO Syūji: *Still Life, Blue*. Lithograph, 825 × 600 mm

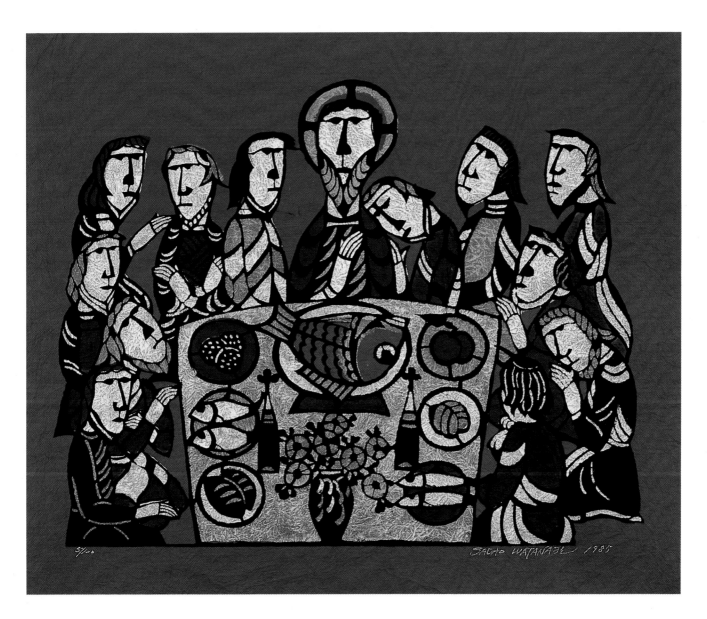

69 WATANABE Sadao: *Last Supper '85*. Stencil, 620 × 710 mm

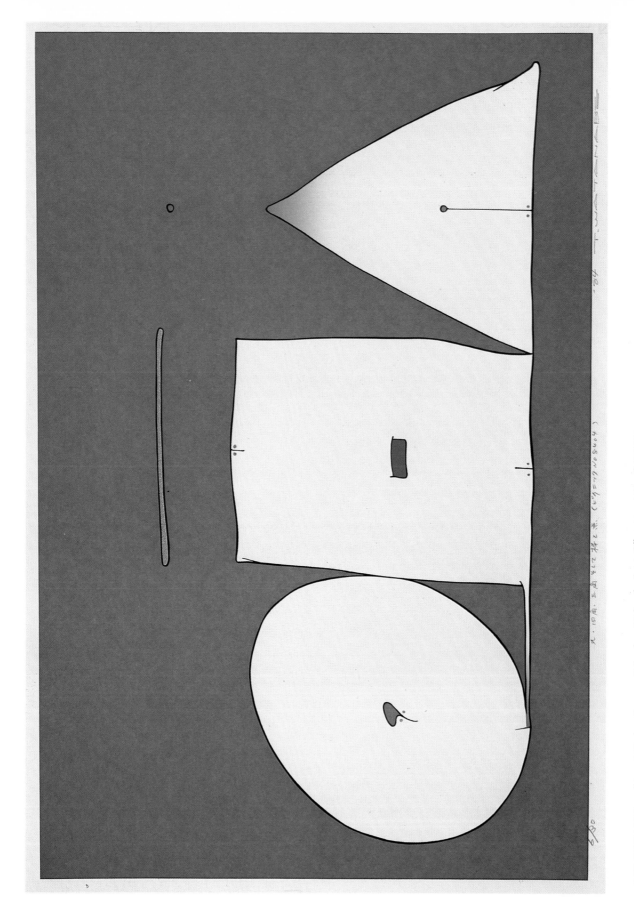

70 WATANABE Toyoshige: *A Circle, a Square, a Triangle, a Stick and a Point*. Silkscreen, 430 × 640 mm

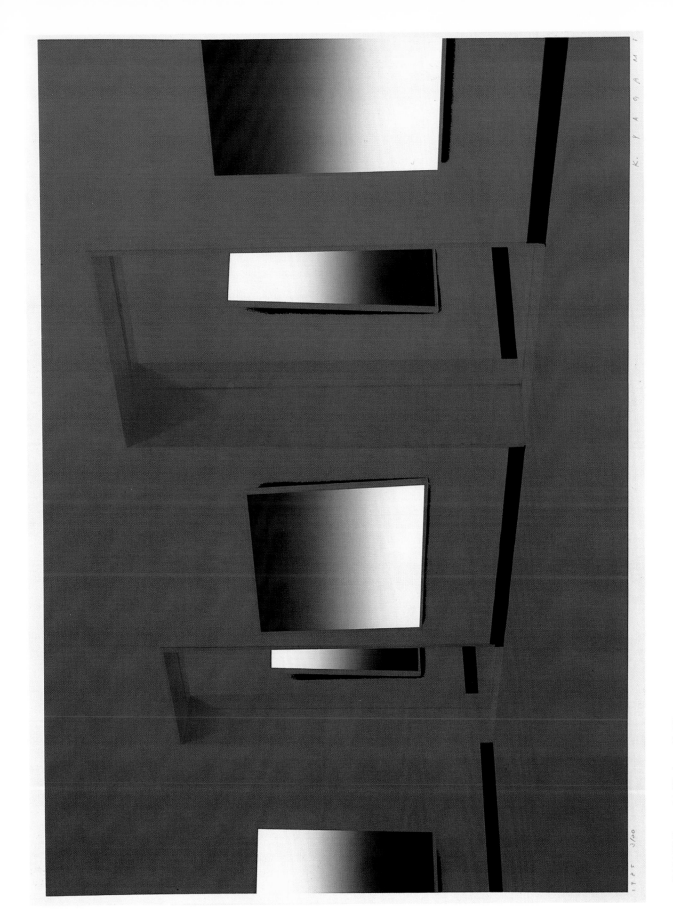

71 YAGAMI Kazutoshi: *Works 42-E.* Silkscreen. 520 × 730 mm

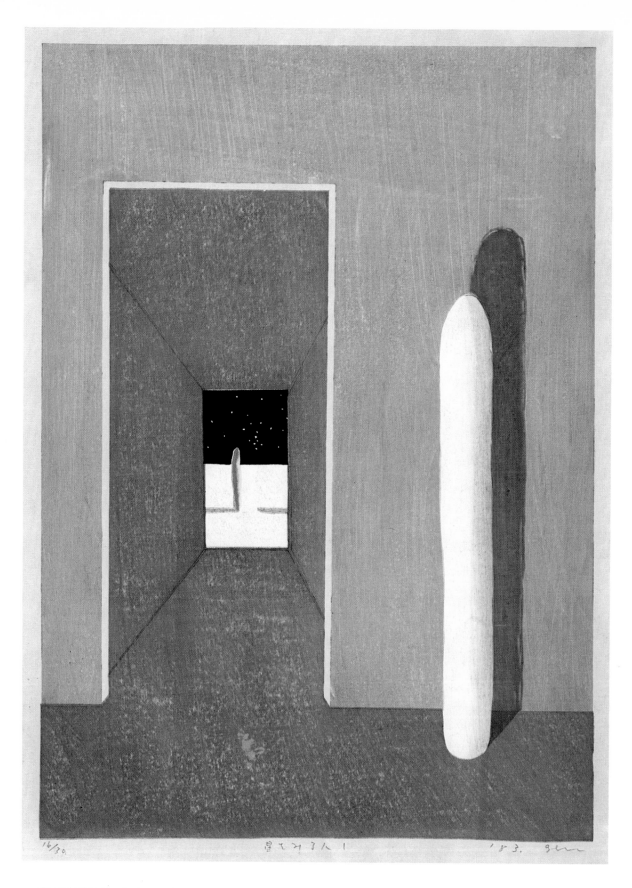

16/30   별을 바라보는 1   '83. gen

72 YAMANAKA Gen: *Looking at the Stars I.* Woodblock, 500 × 355 mm

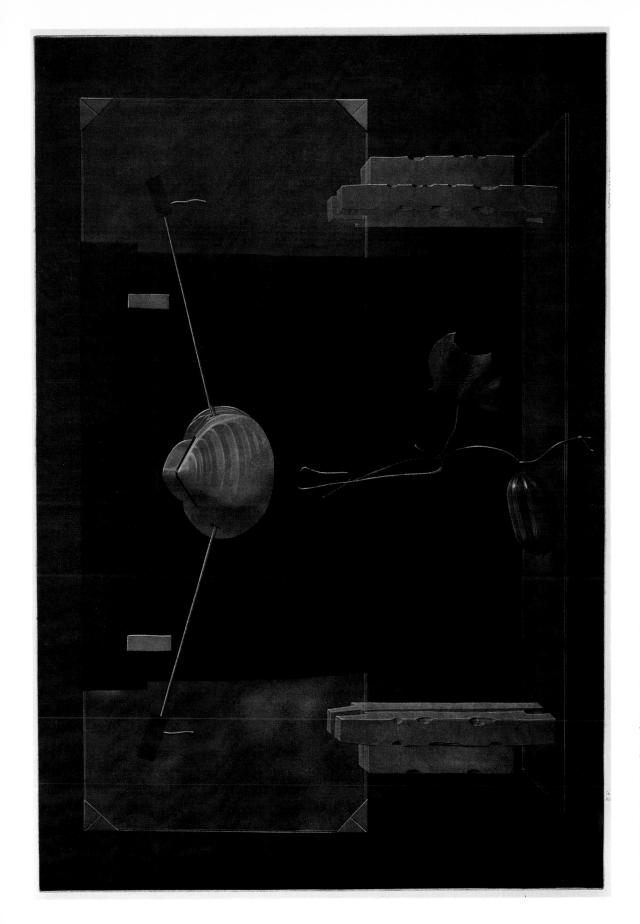

73 YAMANOBE Yoshio: *Crystal Board I. Mezzotint.* 530 × 790 mm

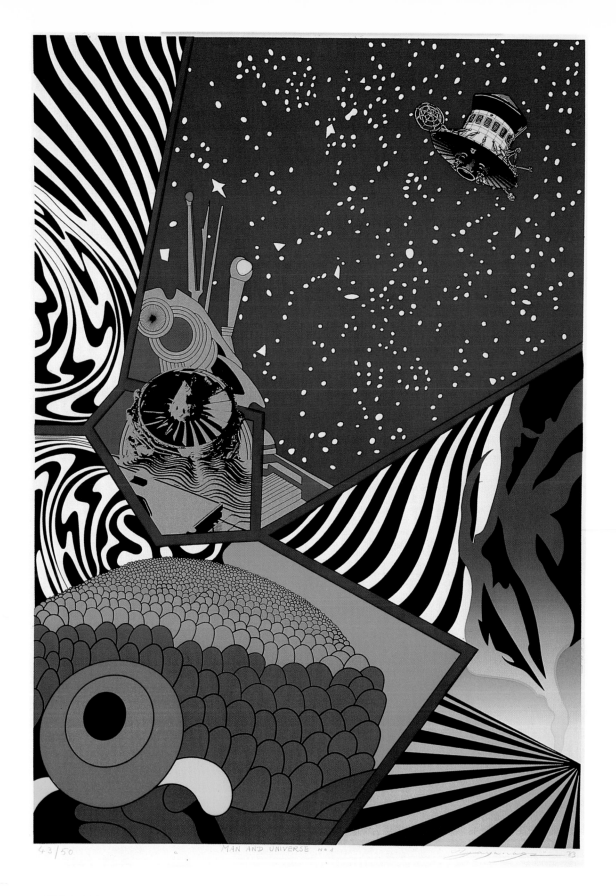

43/50   MAN AND UNIVERSE No.3   '73

74 YAYANAGI Gō: *Man and Universe No. 3*. Silkscreen, 690 × 485 mm

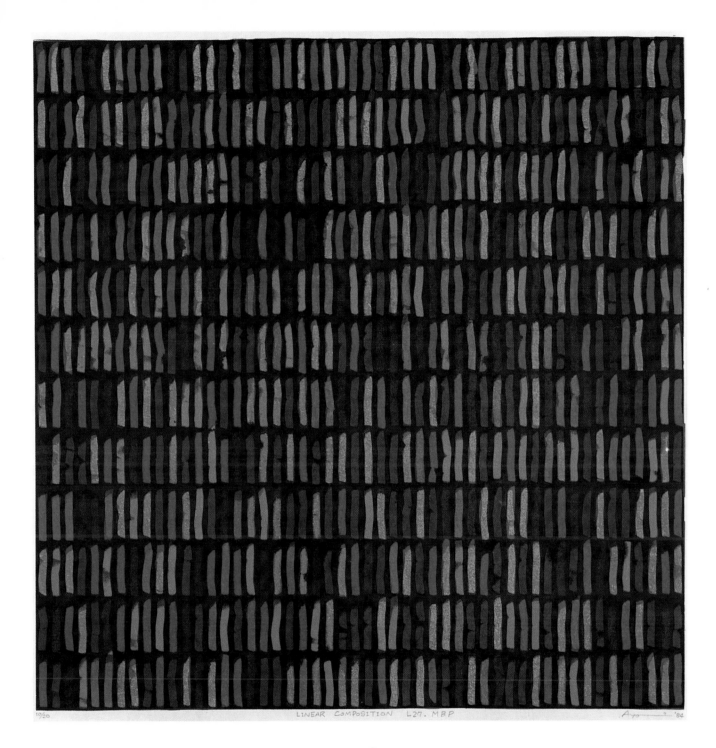

75 YOSHIDA Ayomi: *Linear Composition L27-MBP*. Woodblock, 600 × 600 mm

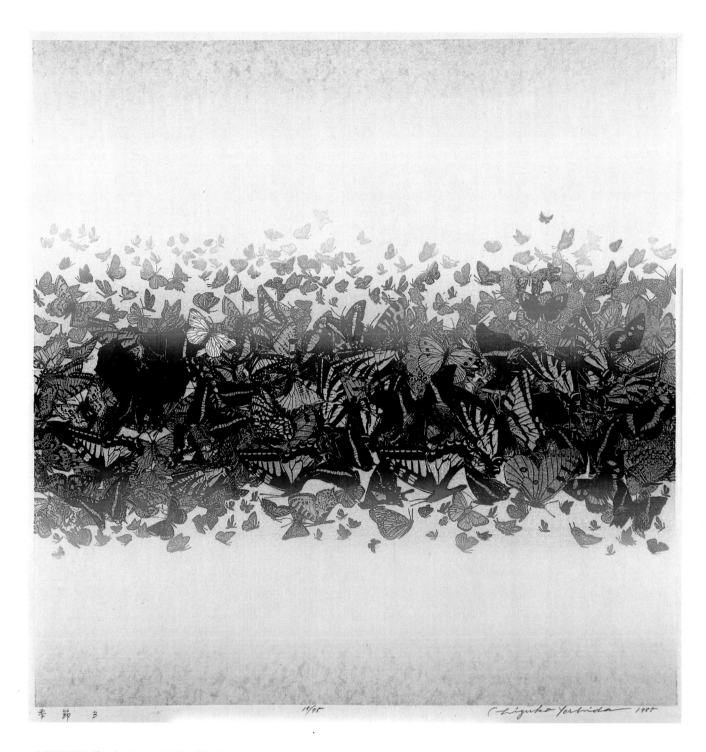

76 YOSHIDA Chizuko: *Season B.* Woodblock/etching, 590 × 590 mm

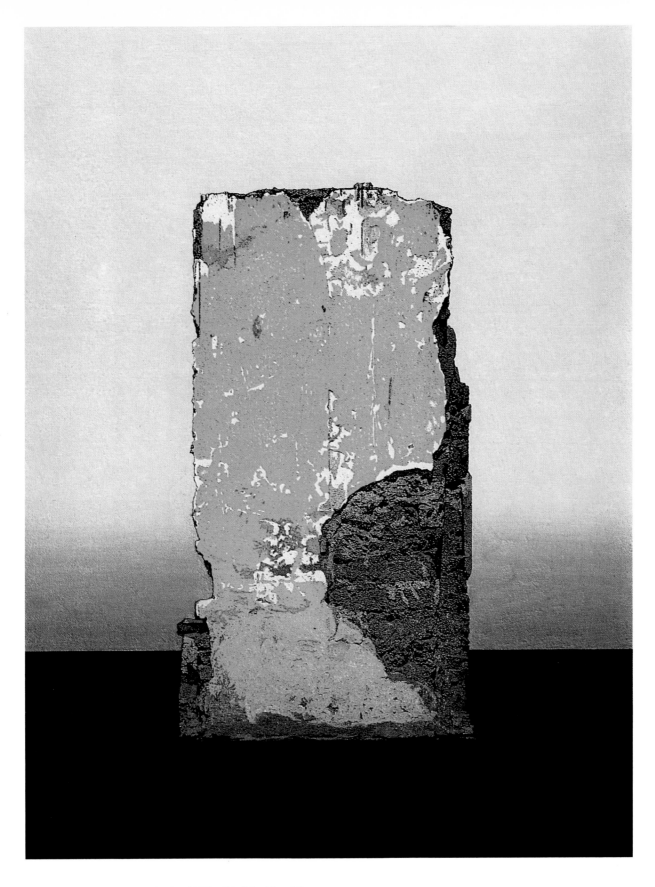

77 YOSHIDA Hodaka: *Green Mud Wall*. Woodblock/etching, 680 × 510 mm

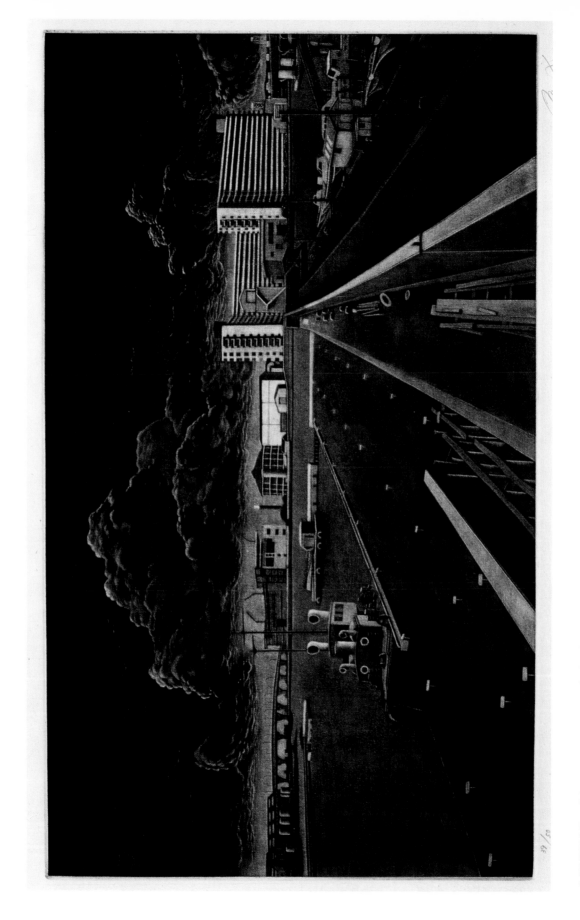

78 YOSHIDA Katsuhiko: *F-Pier at Shinkaichi – Before the Evening Shower. Mezzotint,* 115 × 360mm

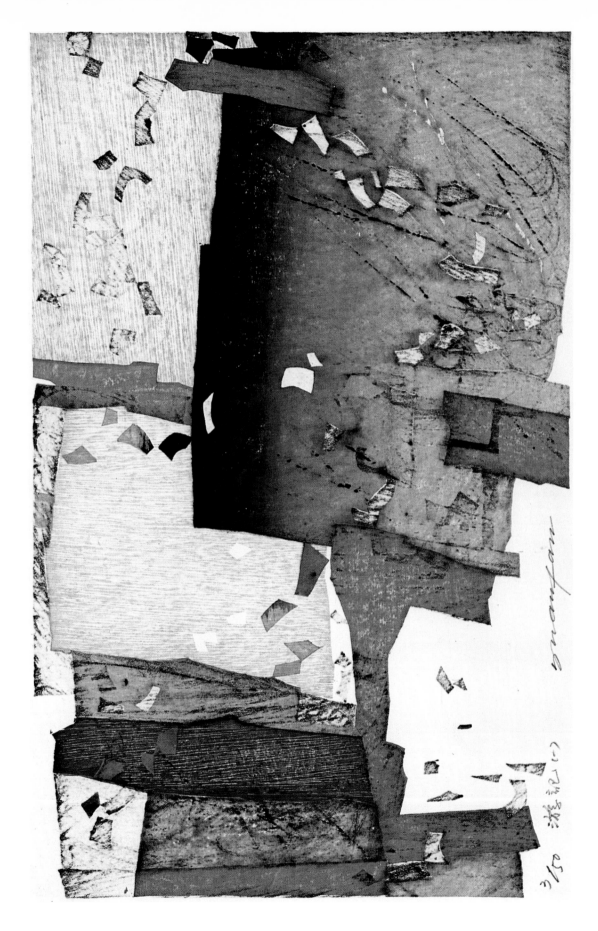

79 ZHANG Yuan Fan: *Travelogue (1)*. Woodblock. 250 × 390 mm

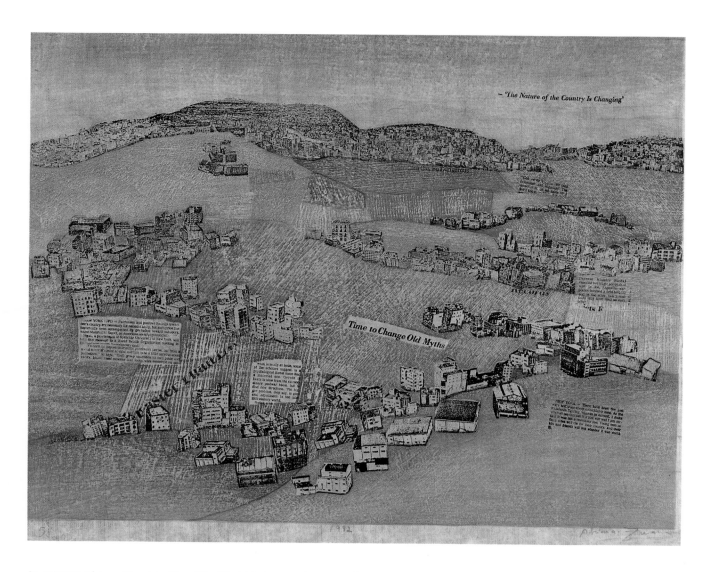

80 ZWANG Adriana: *Mountains View*. Woodblock/photo-engraving, 440 × 600 mm